Southern Living® Quick Decorating STEP-BY-STEP

From the Editors of *Decorating Step-by-Step*

Oxmoor House®

Book Division of Southern Progress Corporation
P. O. Box 2463, Birmingham, Alabama 35201

Library of Congress Control Number: 00-136388
ISBN: 0-8487-2473-9
Printed in the United States of America
First Printing 2001

Decorating Step-By-Step Magazine
Editor: Julia Hamilton
Art Director: Amy Kathryn R. Merk
Homes Editor: Derick Belden
Assistant Homes Editors: Alicia K. Clavell, Alice Doyle, Sarah Jernigan, Robert Martin
Homes Assistant: Tanner Latham
Copy Chiefs: Paula Hughes, Lady Vowell Smith
Copy Editor: Amy Hall
Senior Photographers: Van Chaplin, Sylvia Martin, Art Meripol
Photographers: Jean Allsopp, Laurey W. Glenn
Production Coordinator: Rachael Verschoore

Oxmoor House, Inc.
Editor-in-Chief: Nancy Fitzpatrick Wyatt
Senior Editor, Copy and Homes: Olivia Kindig Wells
Art Director: James Boone

Southern Living Quick Decorating Step-By-Step
Editor: Rebecca Brennan
Copy Editor: Jacqueline Giovanelli
Editorial Assistant: Allison Long Lowery
Editorial Intern: Libby Monteith
Associate Art Director: Cynthia R. Cooper
Senior Designer: Emily Albright Parrish
Illustrator: Kelly Davis
Photo Researchers: Ginny Allen, Laurl Self

Director, Production and Distribution: Phillip Lee
Production Coordinator: Leslie Johnson
Production Assistant: Faye Porter Bonner

Contents

Introduction

WELCOME

At *Southern Living* we realize how important it is for you to come home to wonderful rooms filled with personal treasures. But we also believe that beautiful things can be created as well as purchased, and that's the special focus of *Quick Decorating Step-By-Step.* Our goal is to provide all the tools necessary to make your home an interesting reflection of your own sense of individual style.

In *Southern Living* magazine we've always specialized in bringing you easy, self-explanatory projects for fashionable home decorating. So great was the demand for those ideas among our readers that in 1996 we began publishing *Decorating Step-By-Step*, a newsstand magazine entirely devoted to creative home design, mostly on a budget. This book is in that tradition.

As you look through the pages, you'll find ideas for all of the elements of fine design—window treatments, floor coverings, wall decor, lamps, pillows, tabletops—each with a classic look and a contemporary flair. With a change of color or fabric, you can easily personalize our projects to suit your home. We've also included information on other important topics such as accessorizing and display. The large room photographs provide a wonderful visual resource when you're trying to pull a look together.

We hope that you'll find this to be the most useful book on decorating you'll ever read. Most of all, have fun as you make our ideas an integral part of your home.

With warm regards,

Julia Hamilton

Julia Hamilton
Editor, *Decorating Step-By-Step*
Homes Editor, *Southern Living*

Stylish SOLUTIONS

Want a quick way to make your sofa suit the season?
How about some help selecting colors and fabrics to
create a classic look in your bedroom?
On the following pages, find answers to these and
other decorating dilemmas. The results are
fun, easy, and you can do it yourself!

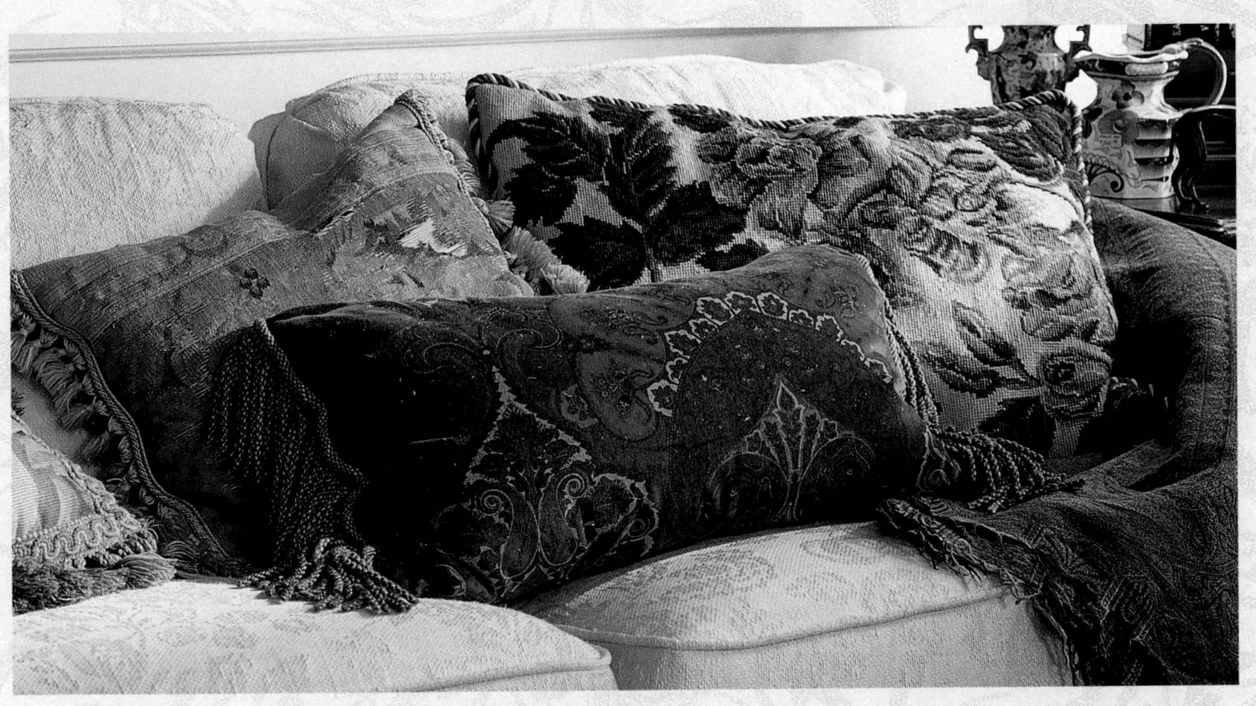

Designer Linda Woodrum turned this second-floor nook into an attractive home office.

small changes, BIG EFFECTS

Q I have a nice desk in a downstairs hallway to use for paying bills and keeping track of household paperwork. How can I keep this hardworking area from looking too businesslike?

A Designer Linda Woodrum of Hilton Head Island, South Carolina, used pretty accessories and creative touches of black to accent an airy writing nook located near second-floor bedrooms. An armchair and spacious tiered desk beneath a bank of casement windows provide the owners an ideal place to read, write, and reflect.

Linda used rustic baskets to hold bills, letters, and accessories to help organize the work area. Wicker hampers placed under the desk offer convenient storage for files and paperwork while making use of open, and otherwise uninteresting, floorspace. A black floral rug edged with a cream border establishes the area's color scheme. Wall brackets, framed prints, needlepoint pillows, and other decorative items echo the accent color, and a simple white canvas shade tied with black-and-white gingham drapes the window.

An elegant lamp provides extra light in this cozy workspace.

The stairway in the home we're planning to build will be visible from both the living room and dining room. How can we make it more interesting?

Architect Dave Davis of Chapel Hill, North Carolina, came up with the perfect solution for Barbara and Philip Post's new home. Barbara says, "I'd been collecting baskets for a long time and never had a good place to display them." Dave made the space under the staircase an important design element by filling it with a grid of boxlike shelves. "The foyer is such a prominent area of the house, and we felt it was important to do something special here," Dave says.

The shelves offer more than just display space. The location not only maximizes Barbara's enjoyment of the collection, but also creates a focal point and conversation piece.

To keep the shelves from looking too boxy, Dave made each unit a little wider than it is tall. He used the angle of the stair to determine the grid's dimensions. The lowest row is slightly taller than the rest to accommodate larger baskets and provide visual weight.

Adding a small mirror in an antique frame helped to break up the large mirror in this bath.

Q We enjoy having an expanse of mirror in our master bath, but I'm sure there's some way for it to be a more attractive feature of the room. Any suggestions?

A For additional impact, designers Helaine Moyse and Patrick Tandy of Baton Rouge sometimes layer a mirror in an ornate frame on top of a wall-mounted mirror. The example shown above makes use of a 24- x 28-inch antique frame fitted with a mirror. The bottom of the frame is 12 inches above the 3-foot-high countertop.

With a lightweight, small frame, a pair of adhesive-backed hooks can be used for a temporary installation. For permanence, have the mirror installer cut holes for mounting hooks before the mirror is attached to the wall.

STYLISH SOLUTIONS

CREATIVE SPACES

Q Our small sun porch has the potential to be a really pretty room. How can we make the most of the space, as well as the potpourri of furniture that will fill it?

A Designer Jane Boatwright worked with homeowner Neal Johnson to transform a seldom-used sunroom of her Charlotte home into a handsome feature. Jane and Neal replaced the awning-style windows with fixed and operable French doors, removed an awkward built-in, and covered the tile floor with sea grass carpeting.

In her travels, Neal has gathered a nice collection of pine furniture in a variety of colors and styles. As a unifying background for the pine, Jane and Neal kept the color scheme neutral by using light walls and a pale sofa. Floral cushions for the wicker chairs, a striped upholstered ottoman, and tapestry pillows add subtle color and pattern.

If you have some old wicker porch furniture that needs a lift, here's a tip to remember. Neal repainted her old wicker in a pleasing dark brown that fits in nicely with the room's casual look.

Instead of buying a matched set of pine furniture, you can create a much more interesting look with unmatched pieces. Here's how.

- Mix pine with other varieties of wood. It pairs well with casual mahogany and English oak. Vary the shades of pine, as well as the sizes and shapes of the pieces.
- For the look of old pine in affordable new furniture, shop for pieces made from salvaged wood. A great variety of styles is available.
- Consider new pine pieces for special needs such as entertainment centers. Pine can be distressed and whitewashed for a pleasing patina.

Neal Johnson's sunroom showcases a collection of pine furniture against a neutral backdrop.

Our compact second bedroom has a private bath that makes it an ideal guestroom, but we'd also like to use it for reading and watching television. What do you suggest?

For clients who owned a two-bedroom house, designer John Kidd of Houston created a spare bedroom that can serve as both a guestroom and TV room. "It was a relatively limited area," John says. "There was no way we could reserve space for a sleeper sofa and get other seating in there. That's when we came up with the idea of having twin lounges made to the same lengths as twin beds." The lounges' tops are loose cushions that were made to twin-mattress size. Large pillows are stored in the closet. And the wall sconce above each bed gives light for reading. The homeowners have enjoyed the comfort and convenience the lounges have brought to the room. "My clients relax on them to watch television and read," John says.

This spare room serves as a guestroom and TV room. The lounges work as twin beds.

ARTFUL ANSWERS

Q *We'd like our dining room to seem more relaxed and comfortable, not just a formal room that's used every now and then. How can we make it into more of a multipurpose living area?*

A Designer Nancy Rogers enhanced the dining room in this new Dallas house by using built-in bookcases to create a library setting. "The idea was that if we designed a library room, it could be used for different things as well as dining. This room opens to the living room. The bookcases also lend a focal point from the living room."

Working with architect Larry E. Boerder, Nancy and her clients planned a versatile space that works as a separate room and as part of the new home's open floor plan. The well-detailed bookshelves were sized to accommodate a French buffet and an oil painting. And the round table, a large dining table with the leaves removed, is now skirted. The same fabric covers an overstuffed living room chair. "The repetition of fabric, along with the cased opening, allows these two rooms to flow into each other," says Nancy. "That's not something you have when the dining room is treated as a separate space."

We plan to redecorate our bedroom but want to choose colors, fabrics, and an overall look that won't seem dated in a few years. Do you have any suggestions?

A For a room that's both up-to-date and easy to live with, try combining clear colors with classic fabrics. That's the approach taken by designer Beth Ervin at the home of Jessica and Grover Maxwell of Atlanta. Sunny yellow walls and a timeless botanical fabric brighten the Maxwell's master bedroom. "We used blue, white, and yellow because they look so fresh together," Beth says. "I also like bolder colors but have learned over the years that when you use simple colors, you don't get tired of them." Walls painted a crisp shade of yellow are trimmed with creamy white molding.

Accessories accentuate the enduring appeal of the room. "I like to invest in accessories and let them make a statement," Beth says. Framed flower prints continue the botanical theme, and an antique porcelain plate rests on a bracket in the center of the grouped prints.

CREATIVITY *with Furniture*

Q *I love the look of wonderful antique furniture but with small children, how can I choose pieces that we can really live with?*

A Scott and Leslie Tichenor believe that antiques and children can coexist comfortably, especially when the antiques are durable, plain-style American pieces.

When Scott, a Louisville designer, furnished his family's combination pool and guesthouse, he turned to pieces he had been collecting for years. "When I first started collecting, people called country pieces like these 'barnyard antiques,' " he says. "They weren't considered real antiques." Today, such folk pieces are prized. They still fit their original purpose of furnishing the rooms families use every day. "It doesn't matter if they get a little beat up," Scott says. "A scratch or dent just makes them more interesting."

He filled the sitting area with American antiques, including a painted cupboard and a Kentucky blanket chest. For comfortable seating, Scott used an oversize cotton check to cover a new armchair and ottoman, and Leslie wove the cotton rug in a traditional stripe. Salvaged pine shutters were fitted to the windows. Other accents in the room include a display of ironstone dinnerware and miniature furniture in the cupboard, as well as a dulcimer and antique twig picture frames.

I want our small bedroom to live much larger, like a master retreat. What do you suggest?

A Joe Thackston and her husband, Frank, have found versatile furniture pieces to be useful in expanding space. Joe, a designer in Greenville, Mississippi, has managed to fit a four-poster bed, bookshelves, a seating group, baskets for magazines, and even a dining table into their 17-foot-square bedroom.

A lateral file cabinet skirted with a linen tablecloth beside the bed helps Joe keep track of her business paperwork. The seating area, with its 5-foot-long sofa and pair of chairs, stands at the foot of the bed. A dining table fills one corner, providing space for photos. It can also be pulled out and used to enjoy a casual meal.

The windows were fitted with shutters and swagged with sheer fabric. "I wanted something whimsical there," Joe says. "I didn't need a whole lot of heavy fabric."

STYLISH SOLUTIONS

DEFINING DETAILS

Q I'd like to update our tiny dining area without making any major changes. How can it become more inviting?

A Imagination can make even the smallest room special, says Charlotte designer Anita Holland. Her own breakfast room is a perfect example of style in a tiny space.

"Though the room is only 7 x 10 feet, it meets our needs," Anita says. "It's a cozy little space with good light." As a first step, she chose a green-and-white-striped wallpaper. "I like to use green in a small room because it seems to bring the outside in," she explains. The Roman shade is a green-and-white cotton print in a vine motif.

A carved wooden planter provides a home for seasonal pots of greenery. It's bolted directly to the window stool (the inside part of the sill). Anita's lighthearted finishing touches include a painted birdcage and a framed butterfly print that she hung from wide paper ribbon. Small French chairs chosen for their scale and open design are paired with a refinished wooden table. Anita painted striped place mats on the tabletop, then sealed the table with clear polyurethane for easy maintenance.

Without slipcovering or reupholstering my sofa, I'd like to give it a warmer, more luxurious look for winter. Where should I begin?

Designer Cindy Smith of Charlotte says to think of pillows as a quick means of changing or updating a sofa.

"I like to point out the versatility of good-quality, solid fabrics for upholstery, especially in neutrals," Cindy says. "Let your color and pattern come from accessories that are easy to change." Just swapping the pillows can dramatically alter formality or impart a seasonal feel.

This sofa, covered in a woven white cotton, provides the perfect neutral backdrop for an array of sumptuous pillows. For an informal, lighter look the designer arranged an antique English quilt with cotton print and chintz pillows. For a more formal look she chose pillows covered in cut velvet, tapestry, and a fragment of an Aubusson rug. Intricate trimwork on the pillows and antique shawl contributes to the sofa's elegance.

Achieving such a rich look becomes more affordable when you look for budget-priced trim at fabric outlets. For maximum effect, apply trim on the outside of the pillow, instead of stitching it into the seams. If possible, have pillows made from down, and vary their sizes as well as shapes. Choose pillows in 18- or 22-inch squares rather than the more common 15-inch squares. The extra size gives a luxurious look and feel at little extra cost. Oblong pillows in a 14- x 20-inch size also feel comfortable.

Though we have a good-size bedroom, the closet in the dressing area of our master bathroom is too small. What should we do?

Perhaps there's an open wallspace in your bedroom where you can add some built-in storage. "One well-placed and well-designed closet can serve several functions," says architect Steve Feller of Winter Park, Florida. Steve designed a closet along a blank interior wall in this room. It's so well planned that it holds an entire wardrobe behind three pairs of double doors.

Because of the location of a window on an adjacent wall, the closet depth was limited to 2 feet. Near the entrance to the room, Steve placed a shallow shoe closet that does not crowd the door.

The design eliminates the need for other built-ins. One of the closet sections houses a wall cabinet as well as a drawer unit that supports a television. A pair of clothes closets are sized for shirts, coats, and slacks and contain shelves for sweater boxes. Racks inside the 16-inch-wide doors keep ties handy.

Panel molding applied to the stock doors adds architectural interest and integrates the closet wall with the traditional style of the bedroom.

ADDING STYLE

Q *My laundry room is so dark and drab that I'm a little discouraged. I almost dread the decor more than the chores! How can I brighten it?*

A According to Charlotte designer Donna Heil, there's no reason for any room, even the most utilitarian one, to be dull. Her ideas for using quick cosmetic changes to transform a laundry area will work wonders for you, too.

Donna turned a bland laundry room into an appealing workspace by using a crisp striped wallpaper, patterned fabric, and colorful hand-painted finishes. She developed a bright Caribbean theme using a few easy, inexpensive ideas.

Donna started with a standard laundry room that had dark cabinets and a sheet-vinyl floor. In its favor, it was a good size with one really nice feature, the arched window.

"I used a blue-and-white striped wallpaper, painted the cabinets bright white, and added blue ceramic pulls," Donna says. The patterned window treatment features a simple design with many potential applications: Fabric panels lined in lime-green cotton are glued to the window frame; the panels fold back at center, revealing the colorful lining. Donna painted the canvas floorcloth in bright tropical colors.

Finishing touches make the room inviting. Airy baskets provide storage, and a small lamp, bright ceramic fish, and a painted stool repeat the upbeat palette.

I'm certain that my small breakfast room could look much more interesting. How can I give it a little drama?

"I like to use an intense wall color and a large pattern—that makes a tiny room more important," says designer Keith James of Little Rock. "When you overscale, there's immediate interest." That's the approach Sally Sanderson took in working with Keith to plan her family's breakfast room.

To give the breakfast area more impact, Sally and Keith chose a floral fabric for the window treatment and pulled the deep-purple wall color from it. In keeping with the room's rich theme, a pair of oil paintings is framed in black and gold. Keith explains, "Heavier frames are important when you are trying to get drama in a space. Details contribute to the scale too." Fringed fabric shades accent the ornate carved wooden chandelier.

I can't decide on colors for my bedroom. Where should I start?

If you're having trouble planning a color scheme, just look in your closet, suggests designer Tony Brown of Nashville. "People usually wear the colors they look and feel good in," he says. "It's just natural for the same colors to work in their homes." When he decorated a bedroom addition for his clients Bob and Stephanie Armistead, Tony selected some of the hues Stephanie wears. "She usually wears soft yellows and ivories, so we started with those colors," he explains.

Tony chose a silk plaid in shades of apricot, yellow, and green for the window treatments. "Starting with fabric is a good way to work because a plaid or a print can give you a lot of versatility," he says. The silk fabric inspired the selection of the sunny yellow wall color.

Yellow satin was chosen for the upholstered headboard, skirted table, and dust ruffle. To tie it all together, Tony pulled the peach color from the plaid and repeated it on the French-style armchair.

Wall-To-Wall CREATIVITY

Strut your decorating savvy, and we'll lead the way with page after page of inspiration for windows, walls, and floors. Stamp your walls with a one-of-a-kind design, dress windows with no-sew curtain panels, and fashion a floorcloth with upholstery fabric. With these projects, there'll be no stopping your creativity.

Getting Started

TOOLS & MATERIALS

- magazines
- scissors
- white glue
- glass or porcelain plates
- spoon
- paper towels

Matchless SHADES

Moving to a new house can suddenly present you with 20, 30, or more big, blank windows to cover in an attractive way. It's the perfect time to consider using matchstick blinds on at least some of them. Because of the low cost of these roll-up shades, it's not extravagant to think of them as a temporary remedy for your window woes. However, their good looks may persuade you to keep them permanently.

These lightweight blinds have a natural color that gives them a relaxed and informal quality, but you can easily dress them up with paint. Hang the blinds from a wire stretched between two trees; then use a paint sprayer to color them to match the trim or the walls in your room.

In the room pictured here, designer Sherrill Holt of Atlanta chose the blinds to soften the light and give privacy. They are usually supported by metal hooks that are inserted in the wooden window facing. But by covering the hooks with decorative plates you give the windows a more finished look. First, purchase wire plate hangers from a hardware store. Insert glass or porcelain plates, and then slip the hangers over the hooks. Adding ribbon or fabric bows that are keyed to your room's colors is another easy means of covering the hooks.

Matchstick blinds are available in a variety of standard window sizes at imports stores and through home-furnishing catalogs.

Cover metal hooks with decorative plates to add innovative style to matchstick blinds.

STEP-BY-STEP

1 TO MAKE decorative plates, cut paper shapes from magazines.

2 BRUSH white glue on printed side of the cutout, and place it (printed side down) on the underside of a glass plate.

3 FLATTEN the cutout with a spoon, and remove excess glue with a damp paper towel. Continue gluing shapes until plate is covered.

(Optional: When dry, seal underside with Modge-Podge from a crafts store. Once it dries, apply a coat of spray paint.)

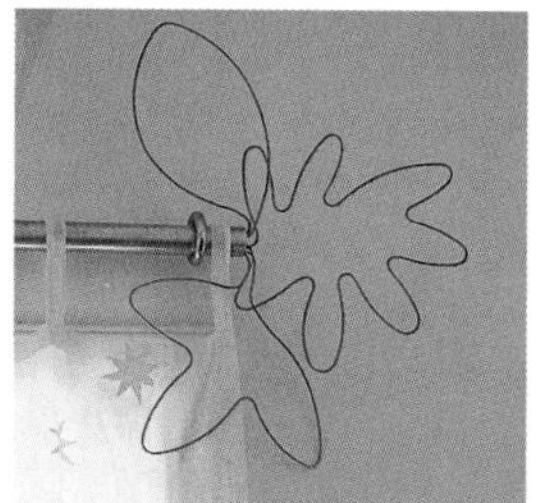

PIPE DREAMS

Turn metal tubing and wire into eye-catching curtain rods and finials.

The quest for interesting, yet economical curtain rods and finials is often time-consuming, and you may return home empty-handed. As a clever solution, try this quick idea for using tube and wire to create shiny rods capped with snappy embellishments. The pairing is perfect for dressing up the simple unlined curtains that are so prevalent in mail-order catalogs and home-furnishing stores. Play on your glittery theme by using glass, silver, or chrome accessories.

STEP-BY-STEP

1 CUT aluminum tube to the desired length. (The rod pictured here extends 2 inches past the molding.) Put on work gloves, and polish the surface and any rough edges with steel wool. Clean tube with glass cleaner.

2 MEASURE and mark the location of the screw eyes, about 3 inches above the window molding. Space them so that about 2 inches of tube will extend past the molding on each side.

3 DRILL holes in the wall and insert the metal anchors. Twist a metal screw eye into each anchor.

4 SLIDE curtains onto rod. Run the tube through the screw eyes.

5 BEND wire into leaf shapes that measure approximately 6 x 8 inches. Leave 3 inches of wire at bottom of leaf. Refer to the photographs for ideas, and be sure to keep the shapes simple. You will need three leaves for each finial.

6 TAPE ends of one wire shape to a piece of wood molding to make a finial. Insert the finial into one open end of the tube. Repeat on the other side. Arrange curtains to desired style.

Getting Started

TOOLS & MATERIALS

- wire cutters
- 1½- x 8-inch mill finish aluminum tubing
- work gloves
- steel wool
- glass cleaner
- tape measure
- pencil
- electric drill
- drill bits
- two wall anchors (for specific wall type)
- two 1½-inch metal screw eyes
- pliers
- 20 feet of galvanized steel wire
- masking tape or duct tape
- two 4-inch pieces of ¾-inch square wood molding

(RIGHT) **Fabric panels hang from a basic aluminum rod supported by screw eyes inserted into wall anchors. For easy finials, bend wire into shapes, tape ends to wood, and insert wood into the tubing.**

IRONED CURTAINS

Follow our simple method to make this window treatment without even picking up a needle and thread.

You can easily create beautiful curtain panels to adorn a bare window. And you don't even need a sewing machine—the sides, heading, and hem of each panel are pressed under and finished using fusible fabric web from a fabric store.

Each panel is made from a single width of fabric. Metal rings with attached clips available at home-supply and fabric stores are used to support the panels. The rings fit over the rod, and the clips hold small folds in the fabric, eliminating the need for drapery hooks or fabric tabs. Artificial ivy leaves attached with small circles of adhesive hook-and-loop tape conceal the clips. The rings, clips, and leaves are painted black to match the iron rod.

tip If you have a wide window, bridge the extra space by hanging two or more panels side by side.

(LEFT) **Allow approximately five sets of rings, clips, and leaves per curtain panel. Paint them to match your rod.**

(RIGHT) **Because the panels are unlined, you'll need to choose a fabric that's attractive from both sides. Gingham, chambray, piqué, oxford cloth, and cotton duck are good, inexpensive choices.**

Getting Started

TOOLS & MATERIALS

- spray paint
- artificial ivy leaves
- metal rings with attached clips
- acrylic sealer
- tape measure
- curtain rod and brackets
- fabric
- scissors
- iron and ironing board
- ⅞-inch-wide fusible fabric web
- small circles or dots of adhesive hook-and-loop tape

STEP-BY-STEP

1 APPLY spray paint to ivy leaves, metal rings, and clips. When paint dries, apply a coat of acrylic sealer.

2 MEASURE from the rod to the floor, and add 6 inches for the hem, 3 inches for the heading, and 6 inches for the fabric to puddle on the floor. Purchase an equal amount of fabric for each curtain panel.

3 CUT fabric into panels according to measurement determined in step 2. Finish the sides by pressing under 1 inch of fabric along the selvages (woven edges) of each curtain panel. Following manufacturer's instructions, apply fusible fabric web under the pressed fabric.

4 CREATE the heading by pressing under ½ inch of fabric at top of each panel. Turn an additional 2½ inches under and press. Apply fusible fabric web under the fold.

5 PRESS under ½ inch at bottom edges. Turn an additional 5½ inches under and press. Apply fusible fabric web under the folded fabric.

6 INSTALL the brackets. Pinch the fabric at top of heading into a small pleat; secure pleat with a clip. Separate circles of hook-and-loop tape into halves. Apply one half to the clip, and press the other half onto underside of ivy leaf. Attach the leaf to the clip by pressing the halves of the circle together. Repeat step 6 with remaining rings. Slip rings onto rods, and hang rods from brackets.

ALL TIED UP

Sew these simple, unlined drapery panels from your favorite fabric.

This easy-to-make window treatment gives a great effect. Each panel is sewn from a single width of 54-inch-wide fabric. A pair is ideal for a window no more than 36 inches wide. Long fabric ties knotted over a simple iron or wooden curtain rod support the fabric panels. The two 94-inch-long panels shown here required a total of 11 yards of fabric. (Because it's unlined, choose a fabric that also looks attractive on the reverse side.) The curtain rod was ordered from a home-furnishings catalog.

The following directions are for cutting and sewing one panel at a time.

tip For greater ease in sewing, use wide ribbon instead of fabric for the ties.

STEP-BY-STEP

1 MEASURE from the floor to the curtain rod, and subtract an inch. (This will be the finished length of the drapery panel.) To this measurement add a total of 13¼ inches for the hem and heading; add 2½ yards for making the fabric ties. The resulting total is the amount of fabric needed for one panel.

2 TRIM both selvages from the fabric. (The selvage is the woven edge that runs along each side of the fabric.) For the ties, cut two pieces of fabric each 45 inches long and 54 inches wide. From the two pieces, cut 10 (5-inch-wide) strips. (Cut in the direction of the lengthwise grain.)

3 PLACE two strips of fabric right sides together. Sew down one long side, stopping 5 inches short of the end. Angle the stitching across to other side; continue stitching up the other long side. Beside the angled stitching, trim seam allowance to ¼ inch. Turn tie right side out, and press. Make 10 ties.

4 TURN under ⅝ inch of fabric on each side of fabric panel, and press. Along the sides, fold an additional 2 inches of fabric to underside, and press; then stitch by hand or machine. Place drapery panel on table, with right side turned up. Separate the ties into pairs; place one on top of another, matching direction of angled ends. Pin the pairs of ties to right side of drapery panel, matching raw edges of ties to top edge panel. Space the ties at equal intervals along the top. Pairs of ties on left and right sides should each be about ¼ inch from edges of panel.

5 MAKE the facing for the top of the panel by measuring the width of the panel and adding 1¼ inches; cut a piece of fabric that's equal to this width and measures 6 inches long. With right sides of fabric together and matching raw edges, pin the facing to the top of the panel, and stitch ⅝ inch from top edge. Remove pins, and turn facing to wrong side of panel. At side and bottom edges of facing, turn ⅝ inch of fabric to inside, and press; top-stitch facing on all four sides.

6 AT BOTTOM of panel, turn under ⅝ inch of fabric, and press. Turn 6 inches under, and press. Again, turn 6 inches under, and press. Stitch hem by hand or machine. Loop ties over rod, and tie into knots. Turn the tie ends in the same direction.

For this unlined window treatment, the white fabric in a reversible tone-on-tone stripe is an ideal selection.

A SHADE WITH STYLE

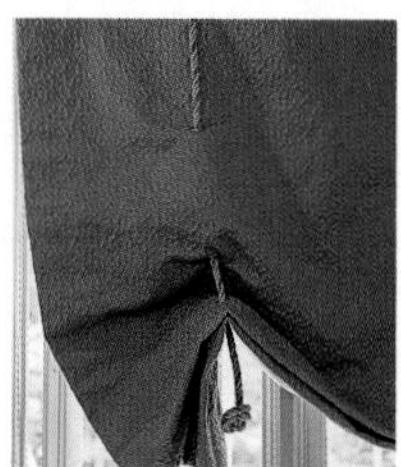

Cording run through grommets supports this simple window shade.

This tailored window treatment is easy to make by sewing a panel from a single width of fabric. It's ideal for situations where there is little need to adjust a shade for privacy and light control. Decorative cording inserted through grommets (small metal rings) holds the shade at a fixed height.

The shade hangs from adhesive-backed, self-fastening strips attached to a piece of painted 1- x 2-inch molding screwed to the window frame. Cording knotted through screw eyes at the base of the wooden strip runs down through eyelets reinforced by the grommets. Kits containing grommets and the simple tools for inserting them are available at fabric stores.

STEP-BY-STEP

1 MEASURE length of window opening and add 1½ inches. Measure width of window opening and add 4 inches. Cut a piece of fabric and a piece of lining to those dimensions. Place lining and fabric right sides together, and stitch along sides and lower edge. Turn panel right side out, and press. Pin top edges of fabric together, and baste. Lay fabric panel on a work surface, lining side up. Turn down ¾ inch along top edge. Place loop strip of self-fastening strips over the raw edges, and stitch in place.

2 LAY fabric panel, lining side up, on work surface, and with tailor's chalk, lightly mark position of vertical rows of grommets. They should be 6 to 10 inches from outside edge (closer to the edge for a narrow shade, further from the edge of a wider one).

3 MARK position of each grommet. The grommets should be spaced 6 to 8 inches apart vertically, and you should have an odd number of grommets in each vertical row.

4 INSERT grommets at marked positions, following instructions accompanying the grommet kit.

5 PAINT mounting board, and attach it to top of window frame, with wide side flush with top. Attach with wood screws. Remove backing from hook strip of adhesive self-fastening strips, and press to top of mounting board.

6 INSERT large screw eyes in underside of mounting board, directly in line with rows of grommets. Cut two pieces of decorative cording to equal approximately three-fourths the height of window. Tie one end of each piece of cording to each screw eye. Hang shade by pressing hook and loop strips together. Then run cording through grommets as shown.

7 RAISE shade to preferred height, and on each side, tie a knot in cording to support the fabric. Adjust fabric to form even folds. Make final adjustments in positions of knots. Then measure 4 to 6 inches down from these first knots, and make a second knot in each piece of cording; cut excess.

A fixed shade made from a flat fabric panel is an affordable choice. Multicolored cording accents the textured cotton fabric. Coach lanterns and a mirrored wall brighten this luxurious bath.

Getting Started

TOOLS & MATERIALS

- yardstick
- scissors
- fabric and lining
- thread
- sewing machine
- iron and ironing board
- straight pins
- needle
- self-fastening strips
- tailor's chalk
- kit with ⅝-inch metal grommets and tools
- mounting board (1- x 2-inch wood strip)
- paint to match window frame
- paintbrush
- wood screws
- large screw eyes
- decorative cording

WALLS

ADD TEXTURE with PAINT

Enhance your walls with the timeless appeal of plaster.

Texture paint enables you to create the effect of plaster or stucco on interior wall surfaces. And it's thick enough to hide minor flaws. Texture paint is available in several thicknesses, so you can achieve many special effects. Use a coarse brush to produce rough texture or a putty knife for a smoother look.

Once the texture paint has dried, paint it with latex. Then emphasize the texture by applying a dilute mixture of darker paint and water. Dab away excess color with a soft washcloth.

getting STARTED

TOOLS & MATERIALS

putty knife, trowel, or coarse brush paintbrushes
texture paint
paintbrush or roller, tray
light- to medium-colored latex paint for first coat
darker latex paint for second coat
natural sponge
washcloths

tip Cut a 3- x 3-foot piece of plywood or drywall. Use this surface for practicing all steps before painting your wall.

Texture paint was applied to this wall with a 6-inch-wide putty knife. When it dried, the wall was painted golden yellow. A dilute mixture of blue-green paint and water was applied with a large sea sponge to stain the painted surface and accentuate its texture.

STEP-BY-STEP

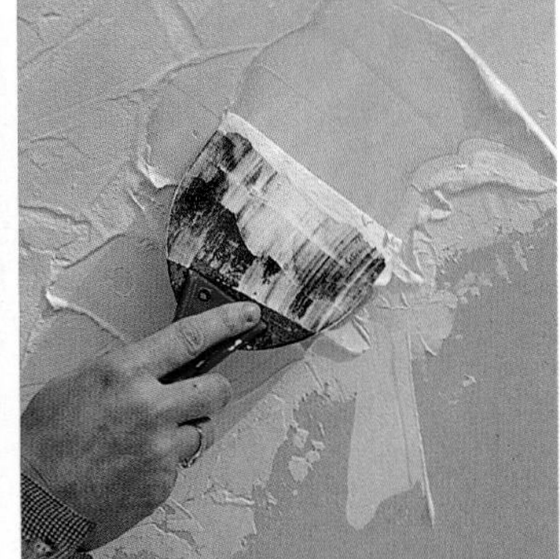

1 **PREPARE** the wall surface according to texture-paint manufacturer's instructions. Apply the texture paint using a stiff brush, putty knife, or trowel. Let dry.

2 **CHOOSE** a light- to medium-colored latex paint, and apply two coats using a brush or roller.

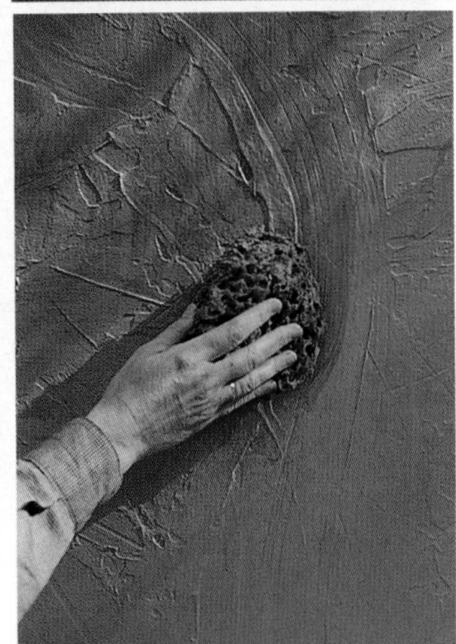

3 **MIX** a pint of water with several tablespoons of latex paint in a darker shade. Dip a natural sponge into the mixture; squeeze out excess. Wipe the sponge over the painted surface. Add paint if this coat is too light; add water if it's too dark.

4 **SOFTEN** the color by dabbing a dampened washcloth over the painted area. Continue sponging the wall with paint and dabbing the painted area with a washcloth until the entire wall has been covered.

PLAIN *Geometry*

Use paint to bring your walls alive with color, depth, and diamonds.

If you're looking for a fresh way to cover your walls, consider a tone-on-tone geometric finish. You'll need just a roll of low-tack masking tape and an extra shade of wall paint to create this terrific effect. You'll also invest a little time and get some practice with your basic math skills.

First, give your walls a base coat of latex paint in an eggshell finish. Then tape off large diamonds, and fill in the design with a slightly darker shade of semigloss latex. The added sheen of this paint, as well as its deeper color, creates interesting effects when applied over the flatter eggshell base coat.

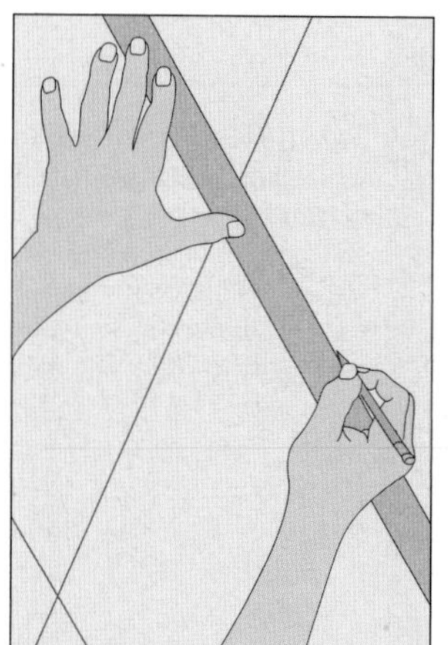

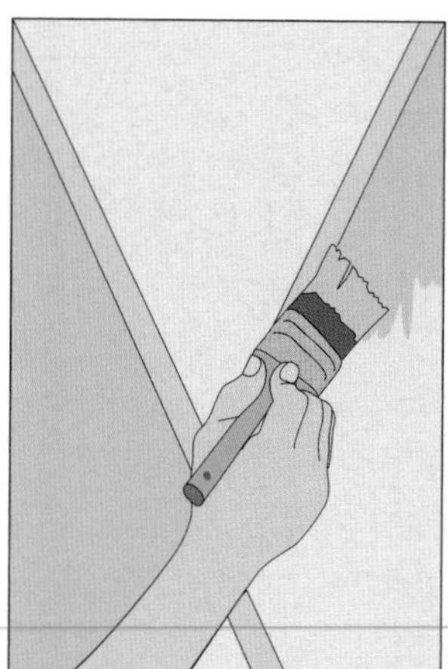

STEP-BY-STEP

1 PAINT wall with the base color, the lighter shade of the two you've chosen. (We used Martin Senour Sauterne in eggshell latex.) Measure the wallspaces, and work out on paper the placement of the design, using diamonds that are approximately 24 x 12 inches. For 8-foot ceilings this works out to be four rows of diamonds. If your ceiling is a little more or less than 8 feet, divide the height in inches by 4 to determine the length of the diamonds. (If you have 9- or 12-foot ceilings, divide by 5 or 6 to get close to a 24-inch length.) Determine the width of each diamond by measuring the width of all four walls in the room (in inches). Divide each figure by 12. If 12 does not divide equally, increase or decrease by ¼ inch until you get an even division. If you cannot get an even division, adjust one or two rows of diamonds by ½ to 1 inch to make the diamonds fit (above a doorway or window is the best place).

2 PLACE faint pencil marks on the wall marking the width and height of each diamond. Connect the dots using a yardstick and a pencil.

3 TAPE off alternate diamonds, placing low-tack masking tape to the inside of the pencil lines. The taped diamonds will remain the base color. With a craft knife, trim the excess tape to create crisp points.

4 APPLY the slightly darker color of paint to the diamonds not taped. (We used Martin Senour Gooseberry in semigloss latex.) You'll need two coats. Carefully remove tape while paint is still damp.

Getting Started

TOOLS & MATERIALS

- light shade of latex paint in eggshell finish
- paint roller, tray, and brushes
- yardstick
- pencil and paper
- low-tack masking tape
- craft knife
- slightly darker shade of latex paint in semigloss finish

Two cool shades of pale sage-green create a diamond pattern above the chair rail in this entryway. A third and slightly darker shade defines the area below the chair rail. White high-gloss paint coats the wood trim.

PAINTERLY PASTELS

Clothe your wall in a creative coat of many colors. Or add texture with one transparent shade.

Are your walls less than perfect? These two easy paint techniques, sponging and ragging, give you a quick way of disguising minor flaws in plaster and drywall. And you simultaneously add color and texture.

At a paint store, choose a color card that shows one color in a range of values from light to dark. Pick the base coat from the lighter values. From the same card select a value several shades darker to use for sponging or ragging. For a more subtle look, choose values that are closer to each other on the color card.

You can combine both sponging and ragging on one wall surface. The multihued effect on the green wall shown here was achieved in three steps. The wall was painted, ragged with diluted latex paint, and then lightly sponged with acrylic craft paint in an accent color.

Whether you decide to sponge your walls, rag them, or combine some elements of both techniques, practice first on a piece of plywood or drywall. Be sure to keep a few notes outlining what you've done. When you return to your project after a few hours, you won't have to rely on memory to duplicate an effect.

With both sponging and ragging you can use latex paint, so cleanup is easy. But with latex you must work quickly to blend edges and achieve uniform results. When sponging walls, especially large ones, let a helper apply the glaze coat, and you can wield the sponge.

getting STARTED

TOOLS & MATERIALS

practice board

eggshell-finish latex paint in base color and sponging or ragging color

foam roller, paint pan, and sponge brush

painter's tape

acrylic craft paint (optional)

acrylic latex varnish

FOR RAGGING:

100% cotton T-shirts

FOR SPONGING:

polyurethane

sea sponge

tip Tape the ceiling, window frames, and edges of trim with painter's tape before you begin. Paint the base coat with a foam roller, and use a sponge brush for corners and edges. Pay special attention to blending corners so that they're not lighter or darker than other areas. Give wall surfaces two coats of acrylic latex varnish when you've finished painting, if you want to seal them.

Three colors combine to produce this paint effect, and it's not at all difficult to duplicate. A rough base coat of pastel-green latex paint was applied to the plaster wall. Then the wall was ragged with a mixture of light-olive latex paint and water. Next, accents of mauve acrylic craft paint were dabbed onto the wall using a sea sponge.

(ABOVE) **The walls in this bedroom are ragged. First, a base coat of light-mauve paint was applied. Then, cotton T-shirt fabric rolled into a tube and saturated with a mixture of dark-mauve paint and water was rolled across the wall surface.**

HOW TO RAG WALLS

1 PAINT walls with a light base color. Mix a dark ragging color with water, approximately three parts paint to one part water. For a more intense color, use less water. Roll a strip cut from a 100% cotton T-shirt (approximately 8 x 21 inches) into a tube. Pour paint-water mixture into a paint pan; saturate fabric tube with mixture. Starting at the bottom of the wall, roll the rag up the wall, using both hands to guide the rag.

2 CHANGE direction frequently so that no pattern appears. Vary the pressure to change textures. Use another tube of fabric when paint builds up.

(ABOVE) **The walls in this living room were given a base coat of light aqua. Then, one at a time, small areas were brushed with a dark-aqua glaze coat and textured with a sea sponge.**

(ABOVE RIGHT) **White bathroom walls gain their unusual texture from blue latex paint applied with a sea sponge. The sponge was dipped into diluted blue paint, pressed to the wall, and then lifted in a circular motion.**

HOW TO SPONGE WALLS

1 PAINT walls with a light base color. In an empty bucket, mix ½ cup sponging color with ½ quart of polyurethane to make glaze. Blend well. Test glaze, and add more sponging color if you want it darker. After base coat has dried, brush glaze over an area measuring approximately 1 square foot. (Working in small areas allows you to keep a wet edge so that you can blend one sponged area with the next one.)

2 PRESS a damp sea sponge onto the glazed area, using different sides of the sponge and varying the pressure to increase the textured look. Continue brushing on glaze and texturing it with the sponge until wall is covered. Rinse sea sponge whenever it becomes filled with paint; let dry thoroughly.

simple STAMPS

Choose fun and fanciful rubber stamps to add pattern and flair to painted walls.

If you prefer walls that are painted to walls that are papered, here's an easy way to add simple embellishments. Use rubber stamps to encircle the room with a colorful band of painted designs placed at chair-rail height (about 33 inches from the floor). Rubber stamps in a wide variety of shapes and sizes are available in crafts and hobby stores, as well as through mail-order catalogs. This decorative band was created with three stamps: a sun, a star, and an S-shaped squiggle.

By using stamps in several shapes and sizes to make a repeating design, you can create an original pattern in your choice of colors. Practice on a piece of cardboard or poster board to determine the best spacing of the stamped designs.

STEP-BY-STEP

1 MARK a faint pencil line on the wall measuring 33 inches from the floor. Draw this guideline on the wall wherever you'd like to place a row of stamped designs. Place a piece of glass on work surface, and pour paint onto glass. If paint seems too sticky and thick, use a palette knife to mix a small amount of acrylic medium into the paint, giving it the consistency of heavy cream. Roll brayer back and forth over a small portion of the glass to distribute paint evenly. (This is important to prevent paint from clumping.)

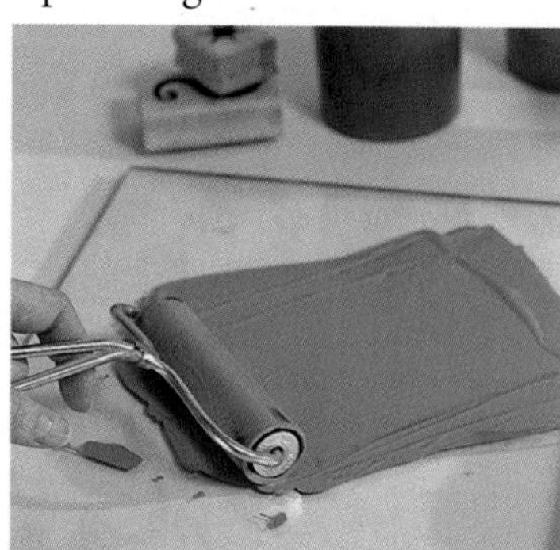

2 SET the rubber stamp on the paint, and then remove it; immediately press the stamp onto wall.

3 FINISH stamping the first color and shape on the wall; then repeat the previous steps with the additional stamps and paint colors. Because the painted shapes won't come out perfect, the designs will have a hand-painted look that gives the room a custom appearance.

Getting Started

TOOLS & MATERIALS

- practice board
- pencil
- yardstick or ruler
- piece of glass (about 9 x 12 inches)
- acrylic craft paint
- palette knife
- acrylic medium
- brayer
- rubber stamps

Suns, stars, and squiggles are a unique source of interest in this bedroom.

ARTFUL EDGING

Make a floorcloth from upholstery fabric.

This quick idea enables you to design and make a floorcloth in any creative combination of colors and patterns. Repeat the fabrics on pillows and cushions for a well-coordinated look.

The following directions are for a floorcloth that measures approximately 54 x 72 inches. Select a heavy fabric for the field (center portion) of your floor covering. Then choose a contrasting fabric, such as a tapestry, to cut into strips and use as binding. Add a few coats of waterproofing spray, and place the floorcloth on a rug pad.

getting STARTED

TOOLS & MATERIALS

FOR FIELD:

- 2 yards of 54-inch-wide upholstery fabric
- scissors
- tape measure
- iron
- sewing machine
- pins
- thread
- needle
- waterproofing spray
- rug pad

FOR BINDING:

- 2¼ yards of 54-inch-wide upholstery fabric (Pattern should run lengthwise; otherwise, you may have to piece together strips of binding.)

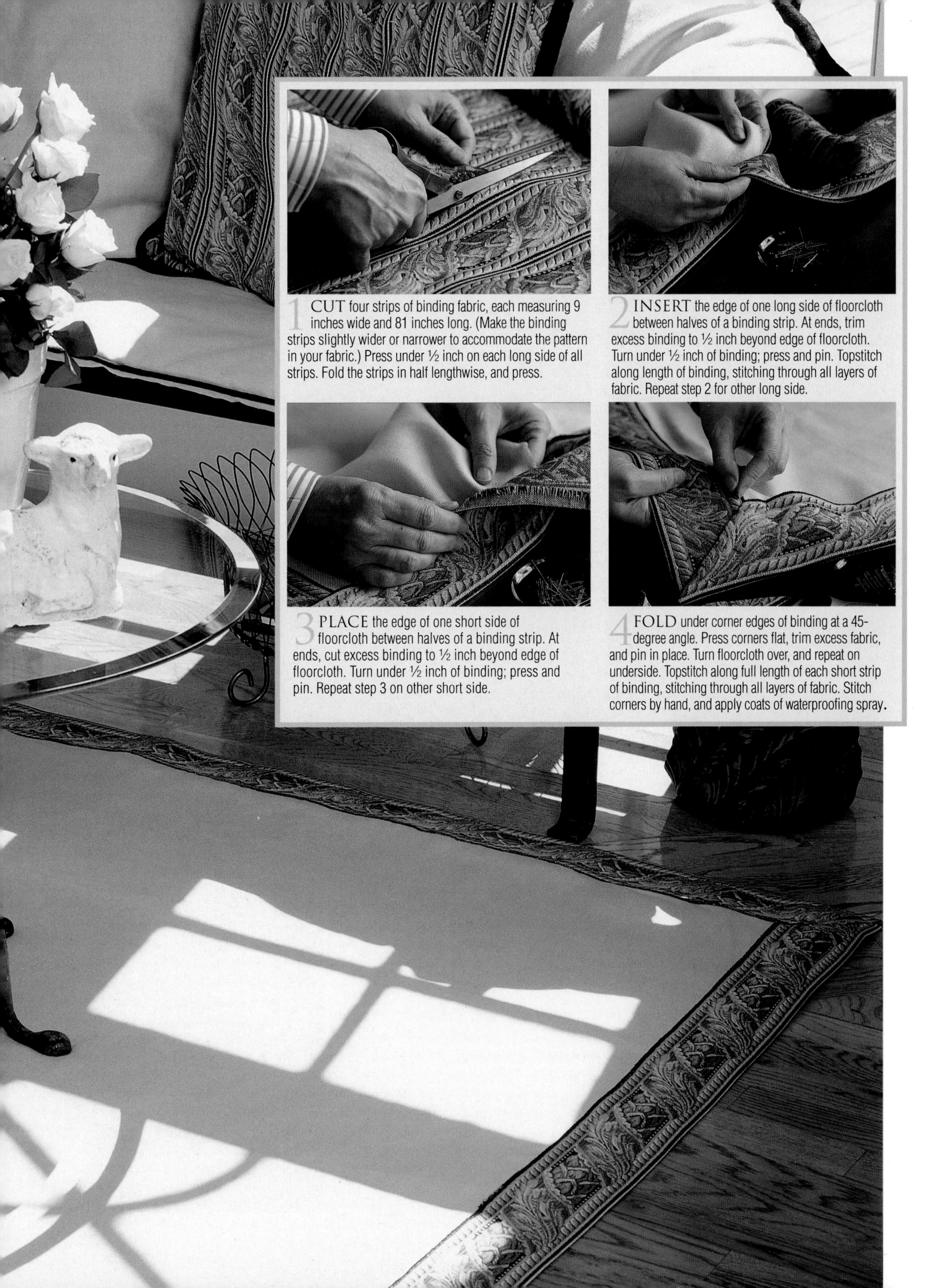

1 CUT four strips of binding fabric, each measuring 9 inches wide and 81 inches long. (Make the binding strips slightly wider or narrower to accommodate the pattern in your fabric.) Press under ½ inch on each long side of all strips. Fold the strips in half lengthwise, and press.

2 INSERT the edge of one long side of floorcloth between halves of a binding strip. At ends, trim excess binding to ½ inch beyond edge of floorcloth. Turn under ½ inch of binding; press and pin. Topstitch along length of binding, stitching through all layers of fabric. Repeat step 2 for other long side.

3 PLACE the edge of one short side of floorcloth between halves of a binding strip. At ends, cut excess binding to ½ inch beyond edge of floorcloth. Turn under ½ inch of binding; press and pin. Repeat step 3 on other short side.

4 FOLD under corner edges of binding at a 45-degree angle. Press corners flat, trim excess fabric, and pin in place. Turn floorcloth over, and repeat on underside. Topstitch along full length of each short strip of binding, stitching through all layers of fabric. Stitch corners by hand, and apply coats of waterproofing spray.

SPRAY ON *Personality*

Add a splash of color to a sisal or coir rug with spray paint.

Adding color and pattern to a sisal or coir rug is easy and lends vitality to a neutral floor covering. Rugs made of natural fibers are economical and come in a variety of shades. Mail-order catalogs as well as home-furnishing stores offer them in different weaves and sizes. Professionally painted rugs can cost double or even triple the price. Why pay more when you can customize a rug yourself with contact paper, masking tape, and spray paint?

step 2

step 4

STEP-BY-STEP

1 TRIM small, medium, and large circles out of newspaper. Arrange the paper circles on the rug to create your design. Three sizes work best. Experiment with placement until you are pleased with the arrangement.

2 DRAW three spirals with a wide marker on the back of contact paper approximately the same size as your newspaper cutouts. Trim out the spirals, leaving a negative shape in the contact paper. Trace the shapes on the remaining pieces of contact paper, making enough stencils to replace each newspaper circle.

3 CUT out all of the spirals. Peel off the contact paper backing, and press stencils on the rug using the newspaper circles as your placement guide.

4 USE extra pieces of contact paper or newspaper and masking tape to cover any exposed coir that you don't want painted. Tape off the border. Apply light coats of spray paint until the color is even. Once all of the swirls are painted and dry, remove tape, contact paper, and newspaper, and your rug is ready.

Black spirals painted on a coir rug add spunk to this screened porch.

Getting Started

TOOLS & MATERIALS

- scissors
- newspaper
- sisal or coir rug
- wide marker (for spirals)
- contact paper
- masking tape (1-inch-wide and 1¾-inch-wide)
- spray paint

Getting Started

TOOLS & MATERIALS

- masking tape (1-inch-wide and 1¾-inch-wide)
- contact paper
- scissors
- newspaper
- sisal or coir rug
- spray paint

A green checkerboard pattern painted on a sisal rug adds just enough color to this neutral sitting area.

STEP-BY-STEP

1 APPLY masking tape over the binding. Then, to create the outer green border adhere 1¾-inch-wide tape flush to the binding. (This is a guide for your contact paper squares.)

2 CUT out squares of contact paper. When determining square sizes, make sure they space evenly along the length and width of the rug, with a contact paper square in each corner (not a negative space) so the design will work out symmetrically. Place the first row of squares the same distance apart as they are wide, butting up to the masking tape. Place the next row, alternating placement to create a checkerboard. Add a border of 1-inch tape butting up to this second layer of squares. Remove the 1¾-inch tape next to the binding, exposing the rug to the paint.

3 COVER the center of the rug with newspaper, and tape down, creating a crisp edge ½ inch from the last row of masking tape. Spray light coats of paint, gradually intensifying the color. When the rug is dry, remove all tape and newspaper, and your rug is ready to use.

PAINT A ZEBRA floorcloth

Answer the call of the wild by making this unique floor covering for your home.

This quick zebra floorcloth lets you add a dash of dramatic pattern to your room. Use it on polished wood floors or on top of a colorful area rug. You can also paint zebra stripes on a rectangular or square floorcloth, or make a runner for a hallway.

STEP-BY-STEP

1 TRACE a grid of 12-inch squares on the reverse side of your canvas. Square by square, copy the outline of the floorcloth from the diagram shown here onto the canvas. Cut the canvas 1 inch outside the outline you've drawn.

2 TURN the canvas right side up. Paint the line down the center of the zebra's back. Then add one stripe at a time, using the diagram shown here as a guide for placement, size, and direction of the stripes.

3 TURN under 1 inch of canvas along the edges. Cut away V-shaped pieces so that the edge will lie flat when turned under. Use fabric glue or a hot-glue gun to secure the folded edge. Paint a ¾-inch-wide band around the edge of the canvas. When the paint dries, apply a coat of clear polyurethane.

tip Contact companies that manufacture sails or awnings to locate heavy canvas in a variety of widths.

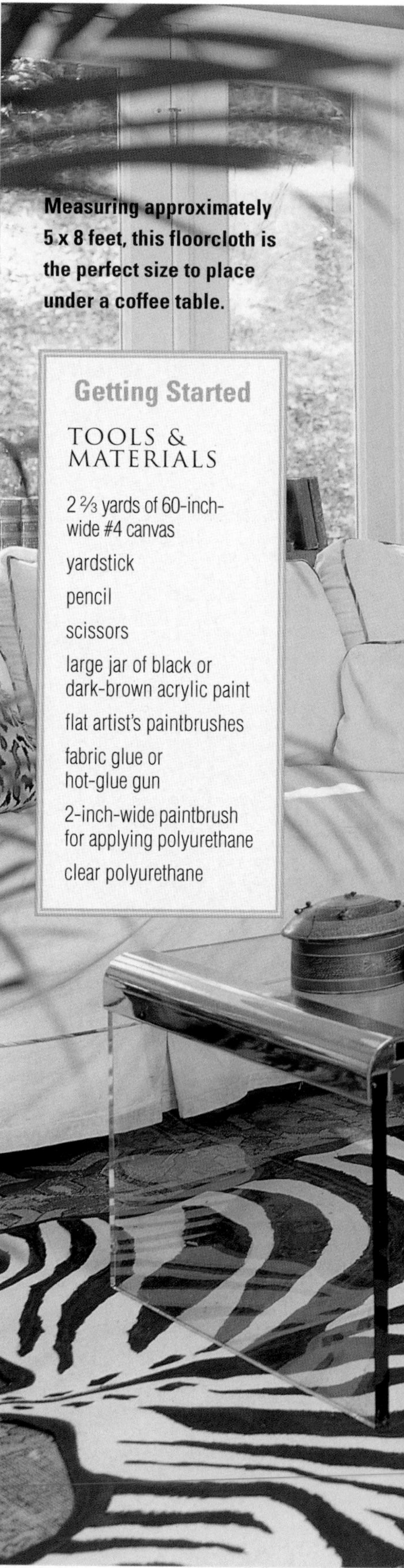

Measuring approximately 5 x 8 feet, this floorcloth is the perfect size to place under a coffee table.

Getting Started

TOOLS & MATERIALS

- 2 ⅔ yards of 60-inch-wide #4 canvas
- yardstick
- pencil
- scissors
- large jar of black or dark-brown acrylic paint
- flat artist's paintbrushes
- fabric glue or hot-glue gun
- 2-inch-wide paintbrush for applying polyurethane
- clear polyurethane

Fun Furniture FACE-LIFTS

Put a fresh face on furnishings in just a few easy steps. In this chapter you'll find ways to transform attic treasures with a little paint and fabric, create custom-colored wicker that's perfectly suited to your decor, and experience the entire rainbow of color options for unfinished pieces.

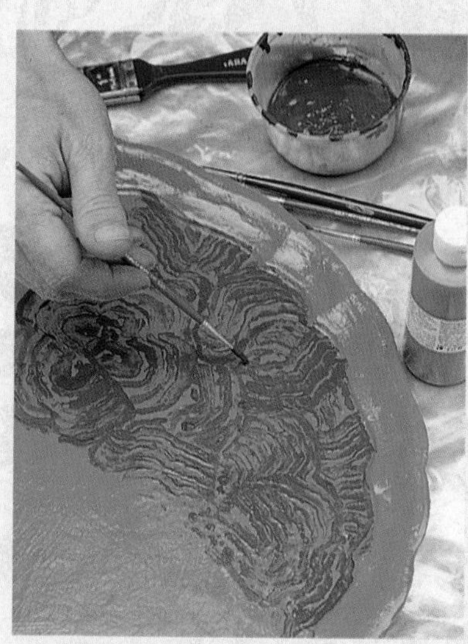

Ivory wallpaper with a pattern of dark-green vegetables and fruit embellishes the doors.

A NEW WARDROBE

An unfinished armoire gains a dramatic presence.

Customize an armoire with paint and wallpaper to increase its decorative value.

This unfinished pine armoire was purchased unassembled at a discount store. You'll find similar unfinished pieces at unpainted furniture stores, as well. Assembling it according to manufacturer's instructions took the better part of one day, requiring basic carpentry skills and a few simple tools.

The overall color of this piece matches the ivory background of the wallpaper; the dark-green accent color comes from the wallpaper's vegetable and fruit design. All surfaces were sanded. Then the armoire was buffed with a tinted wax, adding depth and giving a rich sheen.

The interior side panels (pictured on the following page) are wallpapered and the back is mirrored. Glass shelves provide display space for accessories. Open baskets on the lower shelves add extra storage.

Paint the armoire a color that contrasts with your walls to create a focal point. Or choose a shade that blends with the overall tone of the room. Use the same design selected for wallpapering a room, or choose a coordinating pattern for the armoire's doors and interior.

Design the interior according to your needs. One option is to paper all inside surfaces and use wooden shelves throughout. Or arrange the shelving to accommodate a TV and stereo. For a well-coordinated effect, cover several storage boxes in the wallpaper you select.

Getting Started

TOOLS & MATERIALS

armoire

sandpaper

latex paint, eggshell finish, in background and accent colors

paintbrush

tape measure and yardstick

scissors or craft knife

wallpaper

manufacturer's recommended tools and materials for hanging wallpaper

tinted wax

cheesecloth

baskets

mirror

mirror mastic or mirror clips

hacksaw

4 shelf standards

hammer and nails

8-inch-wide glass shelves

shelf clips

step 1

step 3

steps 5 & 6

STEP-BY-STEP

1 SAND all surfaces of the armoire. Select latex paint that matches the background of your wallpaper. Apply two coats to the interior and exterior. Choose latex paint in an accent color, and give the wooden shelves two coats.

2 SIMULATE the look of worn wood by sanding edges and surfaces of all painted areas.

3 MEASURE the armoire's interior side panels. Cut pieces of wallpaper to fit. Consult wallpaper manufacturer's instructions for the best way to hang your wallpaper. You'll either brush wallpaper paste onto the reverse side or soak pre-pasted paper in water. Apply wallpaper to the interior side panels, and smooth it down.

4 CUT pieces of wallpaper to fit the door panels. Apply wallpaper to doors; when it is completely dry, sand it well, especially at edges. Apply one or more coats of tinted wax to all painted and papered surfaces. Buff the wax well with cheesecloth.

5 INSERT wooden shelves, allowing proper spacing for baskets, if used. Measure space above top shelf at back of armoire, and have mirror cut to fit. Follow product instructions to apply mirror mastic to this area at intervals. Or attach mirror to back of armoire using mirror clips.

6 MEASURE vertical space between top shelf and top of armoire. Use a hacksaw to cut four shelf standards to that length. With hammer and nails, install one standard 2 inches from the back and the second one 6 inches from the back on each side of armoire. Measure horizontal space between shelf standards, and subtract ¼ inch; have two or more 8-inch-wide glass shelves cut to this length. Insert shelf clips in standards at desired heights, and place shelves on clips.

The armoire opens to reveal baskets resting on painted shelves. A mirror is mounted behind shallow glass shelves. The lamp cord runs through a hole drilled in the back.

RENEWED *with* FABRIC

Transform an old cabinet, chest, or table with paint and fabric.

It's easy to add personality to plain furniture simply by using paint and fabric in imaginative ways. This attractive cabinet resembles a hand-painted original, but in reality it's an old phonograph record cabinet that was sanded, primed, and painted. Then a decorative motif was cut from fabric, backed with white paper, and glued to the cabinet's doors. This versatile method allows you to coordinate just about any piece of furniture with the fabrics and colors in your room.

To locate an old chest or cabinet with potential for this project, visit antiques stores, garage sales, or even your own basement or attic for a forgotten treasure. Then select a fabric with designs that are distinctly outlined for the decorative motif.

getting STARTED

TOOLS & MATERIALS

- sandpaper
- alkyd primer
- alkyd paint
- fabric
- scissors
- paintbrush
- white glue
- white paper
- cardboard or plywood
- razor knife
- acrylic medium (from an art supply store)

Green paint updates this vintage record cabinet. A design cut from fabric decorates its doors. Because this project requires few materials, it's an inexpensive way to give an old piece of furniture a new lease on life.

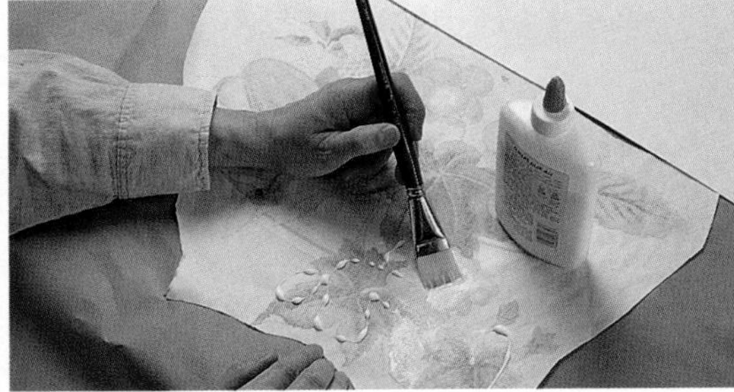

1 SAND a piece of wooden furniture. Apply alkyd primer, and sand again. Then apply alkyd paint in your choice of colors, and let it dry. Sand and paint once more. Use scissors to cut the fabric along the general outlines of the design you've chosen. Brush an even coat of white glue onto the reverse side of the cut fabric.

2 PLACE the cut fabric, glue side down, onto the white paper. Smooth it down. When the glue is nearly dry, place a stack of magazines or books on top to flatten the fabric.

3 COVER the work surface with cardboard or a scrap of plywood. Use a razor knife to cut the design from the fabric.

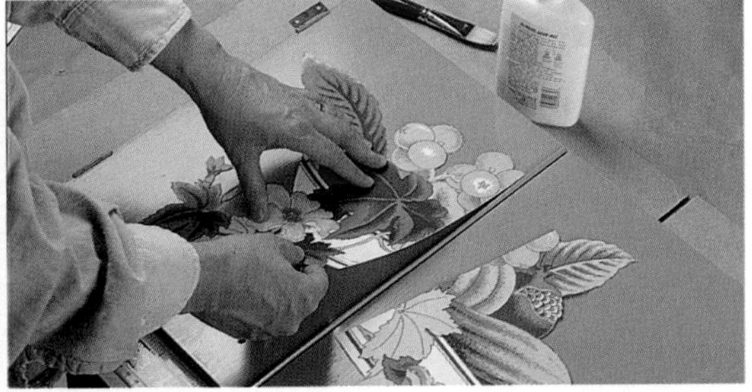

4 BRUSH white glue onto the reverse side of the paper-backed design, and position it on the furniture. Remove excess glue with a damp paper towel. When dry, seal the fabric by brushing on a light coat of acrylic medium. (For ease in applying the design, the doors of this cabinet were removed. The design was cut in half, and one piece was placed on each door.)

CUSTOM COLORS *for* WICKER

Use enamel paint to dress up plain wicker.

You can easily enhance attractive wicker furniture by painting it in your own palette of colors. Choose a set of wicker to paint, or buy a single piece to mix with your upholstered and wooden furniture.

You'll find wicker furniture at department stores, imports shops, and at stores that specialize in wicker products. Select a piece that is already painted or stained and sealed. You can add color to the finish and you won't have to paint the entire piece.

Try to visualize how you can most effectively use the paint. The curved lines of this set of wicker suggested the wide bands of green paint. For added color and definition, the raised edging was painted with rose-colored enamel.

Getting Started

TOOLS & MATERIALS

- wicker furniture
- masking tape in 2- and 3-inch widths
- newspaper or drop cloth
- enamel spray paint (allow an average of one can of paint per piece of furniture)
- enamel paint in an accent color
- small brush with stiff bristles

The paints and the fabrics used for pillows and cushions on this wicker furniture echo the colors in the needlepoint rug.

STEP-BY-STEP

1 TAPE over all areas that are to retain the original color. Cover both the front and back of these areas to keep paint from filtering through the openings. Use narrow tape on curves and wide tape on large areas.

2 COVER your work area with newspaper or a drop cloth. Apply light coats of spray paint. Build up the color in several coats to avoid dripping paint. Allow ample drying time after each application.

3 APPLY light coats of the accent color using a stiff brush. Remove the masking tape when the paint is completely dry.

RECIPES *for* COTTAGE CHAIRS

You can turn an unfinished chair into a vintage relic with one of these simple paint processes.

Today's decorating often starts with a lucky find—an antiques store rarity, a flea market bargain, or an attic hand-me-down. We love to include vintage pieces in our homes for the casual, unexpected presence they add as well as for the stories they tell. Many of these relics wear warm, rugged finishes from years of use; some show off worn layers of paint like a multicolored timeline.

You can also achieve that venerable look by painting unfinished furniture. We've chosen three techniques that work with color in different ways. These variations—all using basic materials—give a new chair an aged, cottage finish. You can modify any of the recipes to match your home's colors and to fit into that niche that's begging for a new/old collectible. Just follow our simple step-by-step instructions for transforming a plain piece of furniture.

Distressing with a Wax Finish

1 REMOVE the seat. Sand chair with a 120-grit sandpaper to smooth any rough edges. Wipe entire surface clean with tack cloth. Apply one coat of flat latex black paint. Once dry, sand with a 120-grit sandpaper. Use a coarser sandpaper (we used a fine and medium sanding sponge) to pull up bare wood in areas that would be naturally worn. Wipe surface clean with tack cloth.

2 APPLY a second coat of paint. Once the paint is dry, repeat sanding process. Wipe all surfaces free of dust. Apply a mahogany-tinted paste wax with a cotton cloth. Follow manufacturer's instructions to buff to a satin sheen.

step 1

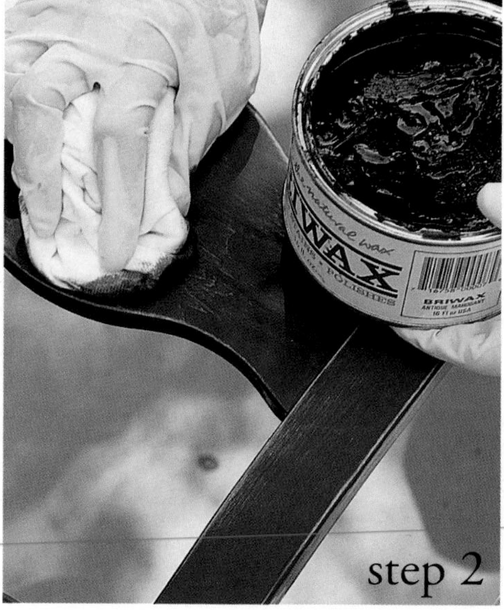

step 2

(LEFT) **For an additional patina after sanding painted surface, rub entire chair with paste wax.**

By sanding back black paint to reveal bare wood, and then enriching the paint and exposed wood with mahogany paste wax, you can make this unfinished chair look as if you've owned it for years.

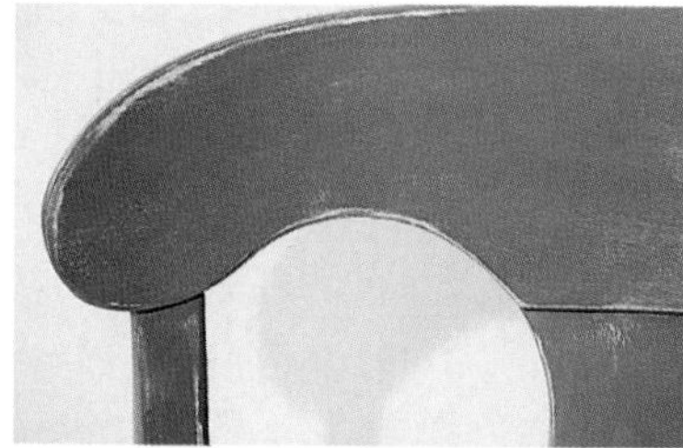

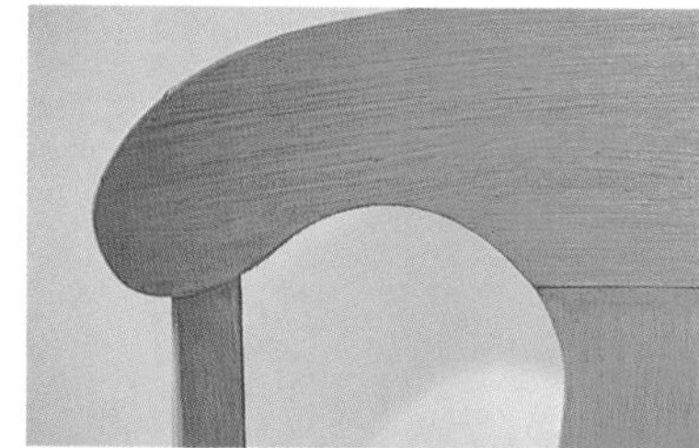

These photographs illustrate the three painting techniques demonstrated in this story: (from left) distressed waxing, layered distressing, and glaze dragging. We include a list of tools and materials to get you started.

Getting Started

TOOLS & MATERIALS

GENERAL

unfinished chair

120-grit sandpaper

tack cloth

2 fine and medium sanding sponges

cotton rags

1½- and 2-inch paintbrushes

DISTRESSING WITH A WAX FINISH

1 quart latex flat black paint

mahogany-tinted paste wax

LAYERED DISTRESSING

1 quart latex flat white paint

1 quart latex flat teal paint (We used Benjamin Moore #664.)

1 quart latex flat green paint (We used Benjamin Moore #650.)

natural-tinted paste wax

GLAZE DRAGGING

1 quart latex satin yellow paint (We used Benjamin Moore #175.)

1 quart alkyd tinted orange glazing liquid (We used Benjamin Moore tinted to match #028.)

mineral spirits

small mixing container

steel wool

alkyd satin varnish (optional)

TIP: It is a good idea to wear gloves to protect your hands.

When you apply several colors of paint and randomly remove them with a sanding sponge, you uncover portions of the painted layers and thus simulate the relaxed ambience of a cottage relic. Our technique for layered distressing shows you how.

Layered Distressing

1 REMOVE the seat. Sand chair with 120-grit sandpaper to smooth any rough edges. Wipe entire surface clean with tack cloth. Apply two coats of flat latex white paint. Sand between coats with a 120-grit sandpaper. Wipe entire surface clean with tack cloth. Apply one coat of flat latex teal-colored paint. Use a coarser sandpaper (we used a fine and medium sanding sponge) to randomly remove the top layer of paint to reveal some of the base coat. Wipe entire surface clean with tack cloth.

2 APPLY a third coat of paint, this time in a dark green. Once the paint is dry, repeat the sanding process above to randomly remove green layer of paint to reveal some of the teal and white beneath. Wipe all surfaces free of dust. Apply a natural-colored paste wax with a cotton cloth. For a soft, aged look, follow manufacturer's instructions to buff to a satin sheen.

In layered distressing, you apply several coats of paint and randomly sand them, uncovering portions of the painted layers to simulate wear.

Glaze Dragging

1 REMOVE the seat. Sand chair with a 120-grit sandpaper to smooth any rough edges. Wipe entire surface clean with tack cloth. Apply two or three coats of satin-finish latex yellow paint. Sand between coats with a 120-grit sandpaper. Wipe all surfaces free of dust.

2 MIX 1 part orange-tinted glaze (start with ¼ of the can) with 1 part mineral spirits. With a 1½-inch brush, apply a coat of glaze to one section of the chair. Following the direction of the wood grain, drag steel wool across the glaze to create a series of straight thin lines that allow the yellow to show through. Work in small sections until the entire surface is covered. Drag the steel wool a second time lightly along corners to remove any buildup. Finish with a clear varnish for protection, if desired.

This paint technique, glaze dragging, starts with a base coat, over which a transparent glaze is applied, and then dragged off with steel wool (following the wood grain) to expose the base color in a series of fine lines. This offers an old-fashioned, hand-crafted look.

RAINBOW color *for* unfinished TREASURES

Wood stains in sherbet shades let you veil inexpensive wooden furniture with soft color.

Using pastel wood stains, you can easily update inexpensive unfinished furniture. Purchase small cans of white wood stain at a paint store, and have each one tinted a different color. Or you can use the premixed color stains that are manufactured by some paint companies.

This hutch and four ladderback chairs were bought at an unfinished-furniture store, and then stained and given a coat of polyurethane. Because the stains are soft and sheer, the grain of the wood remains visible through the color. The polyurethane adds a slight sheen and protects the finish.

STEP-BY-STEP

1 LIGHTLY SAND any rough spots in the wood, using a 150-grit sandpaper. With a dry rag, wipe over the furniture to remove all dust.

2 STIR the stain well. Moisten a rag or sponge brush with the stain; then apply the stain to the wood, following the direction of the grain. Let the furniture dry at least six hours, preferably overnight.

3 LIGHTLY BUFF all stained areas with #0000 steel wool; remove dust with a dry rag.

4 BUILD up the color by applying additional coats of stain, allowing drying time between coats.

5 SEAL the finish by applying a coat of polyurethane after 24 hours.

Tinting each of these ladderback chairs with a different stain adds colorful style. And for an easy centerpiece, set pots of purple coneflowers in an old wooden dough bowl, and cover them with Spanish moss; then add artichokes.

Getting Started

TOOLS & MATERIALS

150-grit sandpaper and #0000 steel wool

pastel wood stains in your choice of colors

sponge brushes and soft rags

newspaper or drop cloth

polyurethane

• Check directions on the stains you buy; they may vary slightly from those given here. Also ask at the unfinished-furniture store for tips on finishing.

Using two different shades of stain emphasizes details on the hutch.

Pastel wood stains are easily applied with a disposable sponge brush.

tip Light stains work best on new unfinished furniture—test first on an inconspicuous area.

A painted malachite finish renewed the top of this gilt accent table. The legs and apron were painted black.

GO WITH GREEN

Use paint to replicate the distinctive emerald-green patterns of malachite.

This painted tabletop imitates a surface covered in malachite, an emerald-green stone with prominent dark veinings. Using acrylic paint and a cardboard comb, you can simulate the overlapping, wavy patterns that are characteristic of this material. Add depth to the combed swirls by brushing on dark gray-green accents. Finish with multiple coats of acrylic varnish.

STEP-BY-STEP

1 SAND the wooden surface of a tray or table, and apply a coat of gesso (an art material that's a mixture of glue and plaster of Paris). Sand and apply another coat of gesso. Apply one or two coats of apple-green paint.

2 CUT cardboard into several 1½- x 3-inch pieces. Make combs by cutting notches in one edge of each piece. Dip a comb in emerald-green paint; then swirl it over a portion of the surface, making a series of overlapping, irregularly shaped Cs. When the comb becomes saturated, discard it and use another.

3 DIP a small brush in emerald-green paint. Connect some of the painted lines.

4 MIX emerald-green and hunter-green paint to make a dark gray-green, a color that represents the veinings that are typical of malachite. Apply dark gray-green lines to some of the outer edges of the C-shaped swirls.

5 REPEAT the painting techniques outlined in steps 2 through 4 until you've covered the entire tray or tabletop. For contrast, paint the table legs and apron black. Apply enough light coats of acrylic varnish to make the texture of the paint unnoticeable. Drying time between coats will be about 30 minutes.

Getting Started

TOOLS & MATERIALS

- wooden table or tray
- sandpaper
- 2-inch paintbrush
- gesso
- acrylic paint in apple green, emerald green, hunter green, and black
- cardboard
- scissors
- small, pointed paintbrush
- acrylic varnish

step 2

step 3

step 4

Easy Decorating PROJECTS

It's a treat to fill your home with beautiful things. And when you make them yourself at a fraction of the retail cost—so much the better. Here, we offer a wide variety of ideas that are sure to suit your style and budget.

ALMOST PORCELAIN

Use artificial fruit to fashion an arrangement that resembles hand-painted ceramics.

Your centerpiece will remain forever fresh when it's created from painted fruit and foliage. You can purchase plastic pears, apples, oranges, grapes, and leaves at a crafts store. Color the assortment you've chosen in a palette that complements your china.

First, give the artificial fruit and foliage a base coat or two of gesso (an art supply material that's a mix of glue and plaster of Paris). Next, use gloss-white epoxy spray paint to mimic the sheen of porcelain. Tint the fruit and foliage with glazes you've mixed from varnish and paint. Then glue each piece to a polystyrene cone.

For this centerpiece, a widemouthed container, such as a vase or vegetable dish, works best. Select one that's about 5 inches tall.

Getting Started

TOOLS & MATERIALS

- container
- cardboard
- ruler
- scissors
- masking tape
- 12-inch-tall polystyrene cone
- artificial fruit and leaves
- gesso
- brushes
- gloss-white epoxy spray paint
- water-based enamels
- water-based varnish
- small glass jars
- drop cloth
- hot-glue gun
- glue sticks

1 CHOOSE artificial fruit in a variety of sizes and shapes. Cut a piece of cardboard that's slightly larger than the opening of your container. Tape the cardboard over the opening.

2 COAT polystyrene cone, cardboard, fruit, and leaves with gesso. Then apply epoxy spray paint to fruit and leaves.

3 MAKE colored glazes: In separate glass jars, mix approximately ¼ teaspoon of each enamel with 4 tablespoons of varnish. Coat fruit and leaves with light layers of color; let dry. Use a hot-glue gun to attach base of cone to center of cardboard. Glue the fruit to the cone, using leaves or small pieces of fruit to cover edges of cardboard and any visible masking tape.

tip Give depth to colors by applying a second coat of glaze.

EASY PROJECTS

a topiary *for* all SEASONS

Try this simple idea for creating a fabulous decoration for a tabletop.

Using a decorative container as a base, you can easily assemble a topiary to enjoy throughout the year. Colorful, dried plant materials—gathered fresh from your garden and dried, or purchased from an imports store or crafts shop—are wired to the moss-covered ball of the topiary and remain permanently in place.

Select a heavy container, such as a concrete urn, clay pot, or porcelain jar or planter. Choose a papier-mâché liner (found at a crafts store or florist shop) that fits snugly into the container. If the liner extends above the edge of the container, cut it away, using a knife with a serrated edge.

(ABOVE) **Hickory branches were cut to form these topiary trunks. Dried ivy, trumpet vine, and poppy heads surround them.**

STEP-BY-STEP

1 IN A PLASTIC bucket, mix plaster of Paris with enough water to make a thick liquid. (Using a flexible plastic bucket makes cleanup easier, as you can pop out any dried plaster of Paris.) Remove the liner from the container, and pour the plaster into the liner. Insert one end of the tree branch. Place the ends of the vines and twigs into the plaster, twisting them naturally around the trunk of the topiary. Place the liner beside a wooden chair on the floor, and tape the branch to the edge of the chair seat so that the branch will stand upright until the plaster dries. Once the plaster is dry, place the liner in the decorative container.

2 PIERCE a 4-inch-deep hole in the plastic-foam ball, using scissors or a knife, and place the ball over the top end of the branch.

3 USE wire florist pins to attach green sheet moss to the ball, covering it completely. Pin thick clumps of moss to the ball at intervals. With florist pins, attach cuttings of dried plant materials beside the clumps of moss. To attach apples to the topiary, insert one end of a wooden florist pick into each apple; then press the other end of the pick into the plastic-foam ball. Attach grapes with florist pins; then cover the plaster at the base of the topiary with moss.

getting STARTED

MATERIALS

- plaster of Paris and plastic bucket
- 9-inch-wide container and papier-mâché liner
- 24-inch tree branch
- twigs and dried vines
- 9-inch-diameter plastic-foam ball
- green sheet moss
- wooden florist picks and U-shaped wire pins
- thick clumps of moss from the florist or your garden
- dried plant materials
- fresh red and green apples; red and yellow grapes

Fresh apples and grapes repeat the rich coloration of dried cockscomb, yarrow, pepper berry, and moss.

NATURAL APPEAL

Give a quick face-lift to an old mirror by covering the frame with dried plant materials.

Dried foliage can bring new life to a worn or dated mirror. Instead of discarding an old mirror frame, cover it with an array of dried flowers, grass, nuts, and berries. Depending on your selection of materials, you can rim a mirror in a palette of subdued neutrals or in a variety of rich colors.

A renewed mirror will cost next to nothing if you collect appropriate materials from your garden or gather items while walking in a natural area. Look for dried leaves, moss, evergreen foliage, lichen, bark, ornamental grass, or any other natural material that has an intriguing texture, color, or shape. You can supplement with dried flowers and a bag of sheet moss from a florist shop or an imports or crafts store. A wooden mirror frame is easiest to use because you can attach materials with a staple gun or hot-glue gun. With these simple steps, you can quickly design a mirror individualized according to your taste.

Getting Started

TOOLS & MATERIALS

- framed mirror
- green sheet moss
- dried plant materials
- hot-glue gun and glue sticks or staple gun and staples

STEP-BY-STEP

1 PLACE the mirror on a table, and plan the placement of the materials. Use the hot-glue gun to attach a sparse layer of moss.

2 STAPLE flower or grass stems to the mirror frame. Use the hot-glue gun to fill in with bits of moss. Add detail by positioning items such as nuts, berries, and small pieces of lichen.

A layer of green sheet moss provides a background for a bountiful selection of colorful dried flowers. Most of the flowers were already dried when purchased, but fresh roses and hydrangeas were cut and hung to dry in a dark location, then glued to the mirror frame.

MAKE A CATTAIL LAMP

Add this bright idea to a corner of your own rustic retreat.

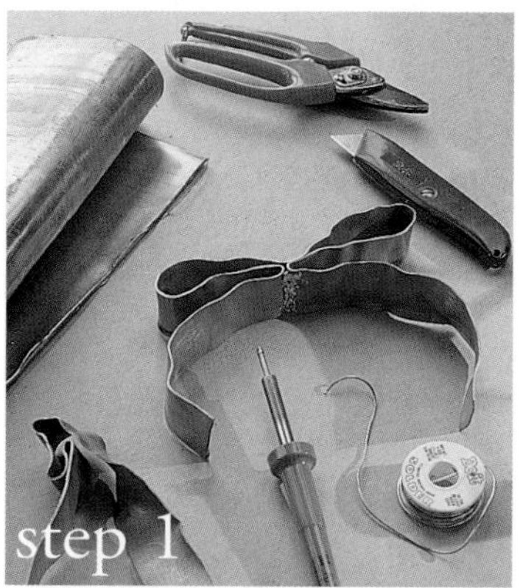

You can create an inventive lamp like this one by adding cattails and a lead bow to a purchased lamp base. The cattails are available at a crafts store or imports shop. You may prefer to use other materials, such as wheat or pussy willows, which also work well. Purchase a 30- x 30-inch sheet of lead from a plumbing-supply shop; then cut it into strips to make the bow.

Have the lamp wired to your specifications at a lamp shop. (It may be helpful to take this article along.) Or look for a lamp base kit at a home-supply center to reduce the cost of the lamp. The lamp should consist of an adjustable rod mounted onto a circular piece of wood with a recessed area in the center. This creates a lip that will keep the cattails in place. Paint the base light gray to reflect the color of the lead bow.

STEP-BY-STEP

1 USE a yardstick and pencil to measure two strips on lead sheet, each 1½ x 30 inches. With yardstick and craft knife, score lead along pencil lines. Place one of scored lines along table edge, and repeatedly bend lead up and down, causing strip to break off. Repeat for second strip. Make the first piece of the bow by folding the lead strip in the shape shown at center of step 1 photo. The bow should measure about 6 inches across. Use steel wool to clean surfaces at back of bow where folds of lead meet. Plug in soldering iron and let it heat up for several minutes. When hot, touch tip of soldering iron to rosin-core solder. Then use soldering iron to heat lead strip at point where halves of bow meet. When lead strip is hot, touch the rosin-core solder to the lead so that the solder flows into the joint.

2 FOLD second strip of lead so that one end is several inches longer than the other. Place fold in second strip at back of bow, wrap it down, around to front, over top, and to back again. (This creates the effect of a knot in center of bow.) Secure knot by soldering it to back of bow. Use tin snips to cut Vs from ends of lead strips.

3 PLACE lamp on worktable. With clippers, trim lower ends of cattails to desired height.

4 GATHER cattails around lamp rod, and tie in place with wire or twist ties. Wrap ends of lead strip around cattails, covering wire. Overlap ends of lead; solder in place.

Create an imaginative lamp by clustering cattails around a purchased lamp base.

Getting Started

TOOLS & MATERIALS

- yardstick
- pencil
- 30- x 30-inch sheet of lead
- craft knife
- steel wool
- soldering iron
- rosin-core solder
- tin snips
- lamp base
- scissors and clippers
- cattails, wheat, or pussy willows
- wire or long twist ties

OFF & RUNNING

Carpet your table with a no-sew runner.

Fashion a runner from burlap and moss in less than an afternoon, and it will soon become one of your most reliable tabletop accessories. The runner establishes a rustic garden theme for a dining table, and virtually all of your clay pots, baskets, and vases will look compatible with it.

Once you've made a runner, leave it on your table from day to day, using one or more plants as an informal centerpiece. When you'd like to give a little extra attention to the table setting, serve breads and other foods from baskets you've lined with aluminum foil or glass bowls, and use clay pots as handy containers for napkins and silverware.

The following directions are for a runner measuring approximately 15 x 49 inches; you can easily alter the size to suit your particular table. Because the moss sheds easily, plan to work on this project outdoors, and store the runner in a plastic bag.

The runner should be several inches shorter than the table. If you prefer, make it short enough to leave room for a place setting at each end.

getting STARTED

TOOLS & MATERIALS

scissors	pencil	newspaper	bag of dried moss
burlap	hot-glue gun	craft glue	twine
ruler	glue sticks	spatula or brush	

tip Add 3 drops of green food coloring and 1 drop of yellow to a spray bottle containing 1½ cups of water. Freshen the moss by lightly spraying it with this mixture.

STEP-BY-STEP

1 CUT a piece of burlap that's approximately 20 inches wide and 54 inches long. Fold burlap in half lengthwise. At each end, use a ruler to draw a diagonal line from the fold to a point on the outside edge measuring about 8 inches from the end. Cut along these lines, through both layers of burlap. Unfold fabric.

2 FOLD ½ inch of burlap on each edge toward center; secure folds using a hot-glue gun. Next fold an additional 2 inches of burlap on each edge toward center, placing glue at the ½-inch mark. At corners, neatly overlap folds, and secure with glue.

3 PROTECT table with layers of newspaper. Liberally apply craft glue to center area of burlap, and spread evenly with a spatula or brush. Press moss onto glue. Continue gluing moss to burlap until entire surface, excluding folded edges, is covered. Either glue down or shake off loose pieces of moss.

4 MAKE a pair of bows, each from several 36-inch-long strands of twine. Wrap another piece of twine 8 or 10 times around knot at center of each bow. Glue bows to pointed ends of runner.

WINDOWS *for your* WORLD

Create your own architectural accent from an old window sash.

Find an old window sash, and you can use it as a quick frame for displaying a group of prints. Or you can create a decorative mirror rich in architectural detail. Measure your wallspace to determine the approximate size and shape needed. Then visit a salvage yard, flea market, or junk store to find a window sash that's the right size.

Many old window sashes have paint finishes that are beautifully tempered by age and use. If you're lucky enough to find one of those, you may want to retain the original finish. But if you prefer to remove old paint, use a chemical stripper according to manufacturer's instructions. Once the window sash is stripped, you can paint it, stain it, wax it, or just leave the stripped finish as it is.

Getting Started

TOOLS & MATERIALS

- window sash
- prints and cardboard
- ruler and scissors or craft knife
- brads and tack hammer
- heavy screw eyes

STEP-BY-STEP

A window sash, with the glass intact, makes a handsome ready-made frame for organizing a group of prints. Pages clipped from either an illustrated calendar or an inexpensive book of prints are ideal for this project. Check the sale tables at bookstores to find books of prints at bargain prices.

1 TRIM the prints to fit, and insert them facedown on the glass.

2 BACK each print with a piece of cardboard.

3 TAP brads into the wooden muntins at 3-inch intervals to hold the prints and cardboard in place.

4 HANG the sash from heavy screw eyes inserted in each side, one-third of the way down from the top.

For quick-and-easy framing, mount a series of prints behind the panes of glass in an old window sash. For variety, leave several panes unfilled.

A slender window sash fitted with mirrors accentuates the height of this open garden room.

DECORATIVE WAYS WITH WINDOWS

- A window with an arched or pointed top will add architectural interest to a room. Check salvage yards for old windows in unusual shapes.
- You can hinge two or more tall panels together to make a handsome screen.
- Window sashes with square panels can be hung on the diagonal.
- Place a mirrored window sash on a garden wall. You'll be pleased with the light and depth it will add.
- Nail a narrow board perpendicular to the bottom of the window sash. Use it for display of collectibles.
- Stencil simple designs on the wood for a touch of interesting pattern.
- Use an enamel paint pen to outline the panes with colorful lines.

STEP-BY-STEP

1 FIND a window sash with the glass already removed, and you're one step ahead. But if the glass is still in place, you can remove it—just guard against touching sharp edges. Turn the window sash facedown on a table that's protected with cardboard or several layers of newspaper. Wearing work gloves and protective goggles, use a screwdriver or chisel to remove the putty or glazing that secures each pane to the sash. Remove the panes of glass.

2 TO CUT the mirror, visit a glass company to have individual pieces of mirror cut to fit and installed in the sash. Prices will vary according to size. The glass installer may use either putty or silicone to secure the mirror to the sash; silicone is less expensive.

3 TO HANG the mirror, have the glass company install cleats on the reverse side. You may then suspend the cleats from heavy bolts inserted at the appropriate locations in your wall.

Getting Started

TOOLS & MATERIALS

- window sash
- cardboard or newspaper
- work gloves and goggles
- screwdriver or chisel
- heavy bolts

tip Hang your mirror where it will provide an interesting reflection. Place it opposite a doorway or window to add movement and depth to your room.

The chalkboard features a little ledge for chalk or favorite photos. Decorate with any wood appliqué you select, such as a fleur-de-lis, fruit basket, or flower.

ALL KEYED UP

Make a chalkboard and give it a trio of handy hooks for keys.

If you would like a convenient place to leave notes and messages, build this quick chalkboard project. It's small, so you can place it in the kitchen or wherever you'd like to post a note.

The chalkboard is made from MDF (medium density fiberboard) shelving that's 12 inches wide. The interesting arch at the top is drawn with a French curve and decorated with a wood appliqué; appliqués are available in a variety of shapes and sizes at lumberyards and home-supply stores. A strip of wood molding holds the chalk. Once the wooden pieces are assembled, they're given two coats of blackboard slating, a matte-finish paint that creates a smooth writing surface. Metal hooks are installed below the molding, and a sawtooth hanger is attached to the back.

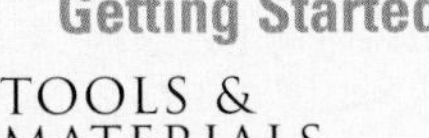

TOOLS & MATERIALS

- saber saw
- 12-inch-wide MDF shelving
- ruler
- pencil
- French curve
- paintbrush
- blackboard slating
- wood appliqué
- sandpaper
- wood molding
- wood glue
- foam roller
- hooks
- sawtooth hanger

STEP-BY-STEP

1 CUT a 24-inch-long piece of 12-inch-wide MDF shelving. At the top of the board, make a pencil mark at center. On each side, measure and mark a point that is 5 inches from the top edge. Use a French curve to draw a curved line from the center of the board to the point marked on one side. Turn the French curve over, and draw the mirror image of the first curve from center to the remaining side.

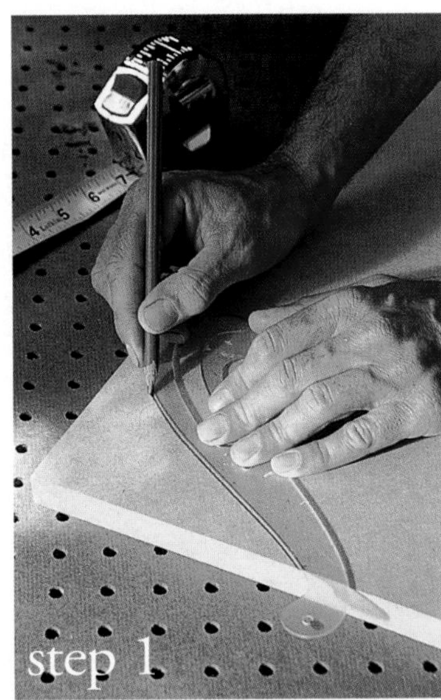
step 1

2 APPLY two coats of blackboard slating to the wood appliqué. Sand it heavily to create highlights where the wood shows through. Cut a 12-inch-wide piece of molding, and glue it to the board, approximately 2 inches from the bottom edge. With a foam roller, apply a coat of blackboard slating to all surfaces. Let it dry, and apply a second coat. When completely dry, sand all edges of the molding and board to give a weathered look. Glue the wood appliqué to the board, positioning it in the center, a few inches down from the top.

3 INSTALL the hooks at equal intervals below the shelf. Attach the sawtooth hanger to the reverse side of the chalkboard, positioning it a few inches from the top and at center.

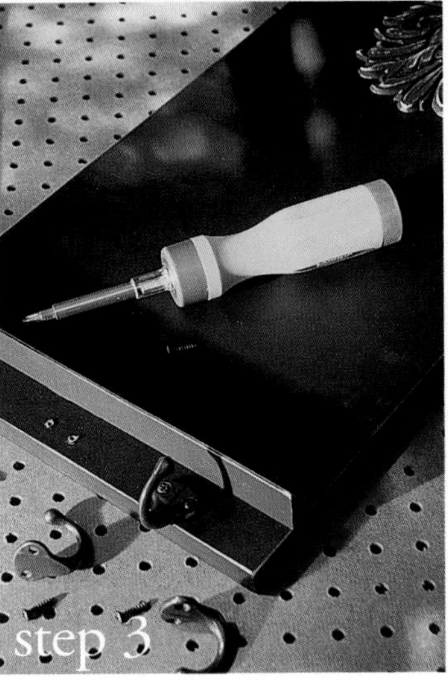
step 3

CANDLE POWER

Cover spheres with flowers and moss for enlightened decorating.

Decorations sheathed in readily available materials—chestnuts, acorns, pinecones, lichens—have a mysterious naturalness, as though they have evolved in some distant and unknown forest.

You can play on their novelty by creating simple candlestick toppers to use in holiday decorating. Cover a few balls to hang on the Christmas tree, or arrange them among greenery on the mantel.

Pinecones, acorns, dried rose blossoms, and kumquats are perfect for adding character to your candlesticks.

Getting Started

TOOLS & MATERIALS

- plastic foam balls, sized from 2 to 4 inches in diameter
- green or brown spray paint
- knife
- dripless candles
- apple corer
- florist clay
- low-temperature hot-glue gun and glue sticks
- natural materials (acorns, tiny pinecones, moss, nuts, and dried flowers)
- individual, pointed, plastic candleholders from a florist

STEP-BY-STEP

1 SPRAY the plastic foam balls with green or brown spray paint. Cut a 2-inch-long segment from the bottom of a candle. Using an apple corer, carefully whittle out a 1-inch-deep hole in the foam ball. Insert the candle segment into the hole. If necessary, use florist clay to make it fit securely. (Don't cut the hole and insert the candle if you plan to place the sphere on a tabletop. Just leave a small area uncovered so that the ball won't roll.)

2 GLUE acorns, nuts, or other items to the foam surface, placing them closely together. Continue gluing until you've covered the entire ball, with the exception of a small area opposite the hole.

3 INSERT the candle segment in the candlestick. (You may need to taper the candle to make it fit.) Use florist clay to keep the ball steady. Insert the pointed end of a plastic candleholder in the top of the ball, and continue gluing natural items in place until the surface is completely covered. Insert the candle.

A galaxy of enigmatic orbs floats above the polished surface of this carved oak sideboard. The variety in the candlesticks adds to the diversity of the display.

Getting Started

TOOLS & MATERIALS

FOR FRAME & MIRROR:

pencil
ruler
20- x 20-inch piece of ¾-inch plywood
drill and drill bits
saber saw
putty knife
wood putty
sandpaper
ivory latex paint (eggshell finish)
paintbrushes
painter's tape
dark latex paint, such as green, purple, black, or red (eggshell finish)
wood glue
paste wax
cheesecloth
tacks
tack hammer
2 large eye screws
picture wire
picture hangers

FOR FRAME ONLY:

6 feet of stop molding
miter box and miter saw
gold paint
small artist's paintbrush
glass, print, and cardboard (10 x 10 inches each)
mat for print (optional)

FOR MIRROR ONLY:

copper spray paint
mirrored glass, 10 x 10 inches
16 large wooden beads

EASY PROJECTS

ALL SQUARED AWAY

Fit artwork or a mirror into a handsome plywood frame.

Using materials as simple as a square of plywood and a couple of contrasting paints, you can easily make a frame for displaying a small drawing or print. Or construct a unique mirror from the same versatile design.

You'll first need to cut a square opening into the plywood; then divide the remaining wood into squares, and paint them in your choice of colors. When framing an image on paper, add a liner cut from wooden stop molding; glass and a cardboard mat are optional. To make the mirror, omit the molding, glass, and mat, and trim the edge of the frame with painted wooden beads.

Display a framed print or drawing by leaning it against a wall or other support, or hang the frame by attaching eye screws and wire. Slip the wire over picture hangers inserted in your wall.

CREATE A FRAME

1 MARK all four sides of the plywood into 5-inch squares. Drill several holes in the large square at center, making an opening for the blade of the saber saw. Cut out the center square.

2 USE a putty knife to apply wood putty to the wood's edges, and when dry, sand them. Apply ivory paint to the entire frame and allow to dry. Then outline alternate squares with painter's tape.

3 APPLY dark paint in color of your choice to outlined squares, and allow to dry. Paint edges to match squares.

4 CUT stop molding to fit inside opening in frame. To make mitered corners, use miter box and miter saw to cut wood at a 45-degree angle. Glue molding inside the opening, leaving a space behind it for the glass, mat, print, and cardboard. Apply gold paint to molding.

5 SAND all painted surfaces, especially edges, to give frame a worn, antique look. Apply paste wax, and buff well with cheesecloth.

6 PLACE glass, mat, print, and cardboard backing behind stop molding, and secure them by inserting several tacks into the wood.

7 ATTACH eye screws on left and right of reverse side of frame, approximately 6 inches from the top. Cut a 30-inch piece of picture wire, and run it through the eye screws. Twist the ends back around the center section of wire and hang from picture hangers inserted in wall.

MAKE A MIRROR

1 FOLLOW steps 1 through 7 for creating the frame, but omit steps 4 and 6.

2 SPRAY the tacks with copper paint. Place the mirrored glass in the opening. Secure it by placing one tack at center of each of the four sides, both in front of the mirror and behind it.

3 APPLY copper spray paint to the wooden beads, and glue them to edge of frame, placing one at the center of each square.

step 2

step 3

step 4

step 5

EASY PROJECTS

MOSAIC tables

In several easy steps, cover the top of a table with decorative tile or broken china.

Since ancient times, artists have created images by arranging small pieces of colored glass and tile to form mosaics. Using this same technique, you can cover a tabletop with fragments of ceramic tile or porcelain plates.

First, select a table. Unfinished-furniture stores are a good source for small end tables at reasonable prices. From a tile store, purchase enough 4- x 4-inch tiles to cover the top of your table. (To be sure, buy a few extra tiles.) Or if you prefer to cover the tabletop with broken china, check flea markets and second-hand stores for plates and platters. Flat pieces from the base of a plate are best; the curved rims must be broken into smaller fragments to lie flat. If sharp edges of tile or china protrude from the grout, have a piece of glass cut to cover the tabletop.

tip Use grout in premixed colors or customize white grout by adding artist's acrylic paints.

STEP-BY-STEP

1 MEASURE the tabletop, and cut wood molding to fit. Cut the end of each piece at a 45-degree angle so that you can miter the corners by fitting the molding together to form a 90-degree angle. (A miter box is helpful, but not necessary, for making angled cuts.) Using wood glue and small finishing nails, attach the molding to the tabletop.

2 PROTECT your eyes by wearing goggles. Wrap a tile or plate in a dish towel, place it facedown on a flat surface, and break it into several pieces with a small mallet or hammer. Using an adhesive spreader with notched edges, spread a layer of ceramic tile adhesive over a portion of the tabletop.

3 PRESS pieces of broken ceramic tile into the adhesive. Continue applying adhesive and tile until the tabletop is covered. Let it dry for 24 hours. If you're using china fragments, apply a thicker bed of adhesive because the pieces aren't flat. It will take longer for thicker adhesive to dry, so be sure to allow extra drying time.

4 MIX the grout with water, following manufacturer's instructions. With the trowel, spread the grout over the table surface, and press it down into spaces between fragments of tile and china.

5 REMOVE excess grout with a damp sponge.

6 REMOVE grout residue when dry by polishing the surface of the tile or china with an abrasive pad.

7 PAINT or stain the wood table. This table was stained using artist's oil paint. A bit of black paint was applied to a sponge moistened with turpentine. Then the paint was rubbed into the wood.

An unfinished table was edged with molding and then topped with fragments of ceramic tile. Grout fills the spaces between the fragments.

Getting Started

TOOLS & MATERIALS

- wooden table
- ruler or yardstick
- narrow wood molding for edging tabletop (purchase a few extra feet)
- wood glue
- small finishing nails
- saw
- protective goggles
- porcelain plates or ceramic tile
- dish towel
- mallet or hammer
- paint or stain
- sponge

FROM A CERAMIC TILE SUPPLIER:

- tile adhesive
- adhesive spreader with notched edge
- grout and abrasive pad
- trowel

REVAMP YOUR LAMPS

Transform a ho-hum lamp into an enlightened accessory.

Enhance the overall appearance of your room with a distinctive accent—a lamp that you've painted by hand. Though the results are quite spectacular, this is an easy project.

Start with a white ginger jar lamp, the kind that's sold at home-supply stores, and embellish it with no-bake enamel paint from an art-supply store. Choose a shade that relates to your room's color scheme, and apply paints in a simple geometric or floral pattern.

Getting Started

TOOLS & MATERIALS

- ceramic lamp
- ceramic finial
- denatured alcohol or Delta CeramDecor Air-Dry Perm Enamel Surface Conditioner
- cotton rags
- paintbrushes in several sizes
- Delta CeramDecor Air-Dry PermEnamel in several colors
- Delta CeramDecor Air-Dry Perm Enamel Clear Satin Glaze

STEP-BY-STEP

1 CLEAN all ceramic surfaces with denatured alcohol or Surface Conditioner. Apply the background color to the larger areas, and allow to dry. Don't be concerned if the paint is not completely opaque; a more varied painterly look will give the design character (besides, you can always apply more paint for extra coverage). Paint any additional details on the body of the lamp, and allow to dry.

2 PAINT the base and top of the lamp, then choose and apply an accent color to the finial. When the paint is completely dry, apply a coat of clear gloss glaze to the entire lamp and the finial. Allow paint to harden 24 hours before transporting to purchase a shade.

tip If you begin painting and are not pleased with the color or design, wash the paint off before it hardens, and start over. You'll need to clean the surface again with alcohol.

Bright greens and yellows form a plaid design and coordinate with the pillow fabric and wall color.

SELECTING A SHADE

Cap your new painted lamp base with the perfect shade. For timeless beauty, lampshades with classic lines and proportions are favored over unusual, trendy styles, and shades made of silk or heavy parchment always provide a look of high quality. White shades usually reflect the most light, and black shades add drama and give a more delicate glow. Tan and off-white lampshades create softness, and gold-lined shades offer additional warmth. A three-way socket or dimming knob adds ambience with just a turn of the switch.

The harp (the metal frame that holds the shade) can be replaced to adjust the overall height of a lamp. The shade should cover the socket but not detract from the base, and electric cords should be a color that will recede against the wall or floor. Think of the finial, especially one used on a lamp set on a low table, as the crowning touch.

A grouping of three finials varying in their neutral tones adds a touch of elegance to this desktop.

E A S Y   P R O J E C T S

CROWNING DETAILS

Make indoor accents with outdoor architectural elements.

The graceful lines of these exterior architectural finials are so beautiful that they deserve to come inside. Finished in a Craquelure varnish to give an authentic antique look, and enhanced with a tinted wax, they make a nice addition to a mantel, desktop, or bookshelf.

Purchase wood finials in any size or shape. Groupings of two or three are especially attractive. Prepare the surface by sanding; then finish with an easy latex crackle varnish. This simple technique gives a handsome look.

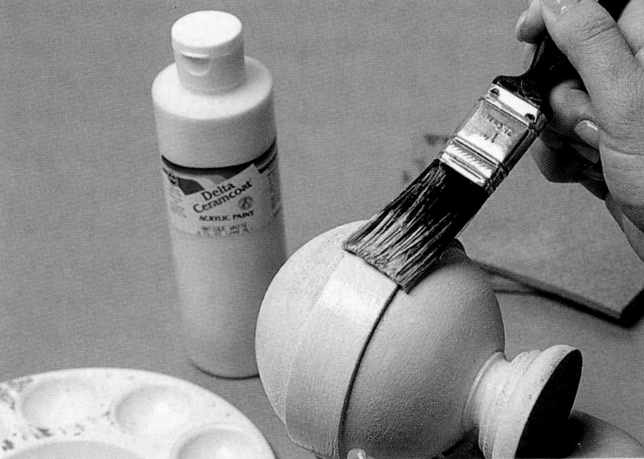

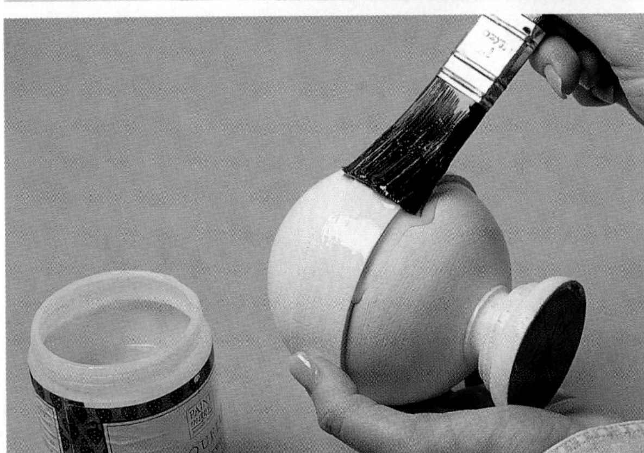

Getting Started

TOOLS & MATERIALS

- finials
- medium-fine grade sanding sponges
- tack cloth
- small bottle of acrylic primer
- acrylic craft paint
- 1½-inch paintbrush
- Paint Magic Craquelure Varnish kit
- tinted paste wax
- rags

STEP-BY-STEP

1 SAND the finial until the surface is very smooth. Remove all dust particles with a tack cloth. Apply a coat of primer to seal the porous wood. Allow to dry, and sand lightly. Next, apply two to three coats of acrylic paint in a color of your choice. Allow one hour of drying time between each coat, and sand lightly each time. After your final coat, allow to dry several hours.

2 FOLLOWING manufacturer's instructions, apply the two-step Craquelure varnish. You will see the cracks appear once the varnish dries.

3 RUB on tinted paste wax with a soft cloth (we used a mahogany tint), letting the wax fill the cracks. Wait a few minutes, and buff to a low sheen.

4 ADD a base to the finial for extra emphasis. Your local lamp shop can make bases in varying sizes and finish them in several stains. The cost will vary depending on size.

REST EASY

It's surprisingly easy to build your own custom headboard using plywood, padding, and fabric.

A new headboard will make a great starting point for redecorating your bedroom. Cover it in your choice of heavy fabrics, or use a fragment of a lightweight rug. A fragment of a damaged Turkish rug was just large enough to upholster this headboard. The pillows were chosen at a home-furnishings store for their correlating colors and patterns.

STEP-BY-STEP

1 USE the width of a 4- x 8-foot sheet of plywood as the height of your headboard (48 inches). Cut the length of the plywood to equal the width of your mattress (52 inches for full, 60 inches for queen, and 70 inches for king). Or you can make the headboard a few inches wider. Nail two 1 x 4s to the back of the headboard, positioning them vertically, about 1 foot from the outside edges.

2 CREATE curved edges at top by tracing around a dinner plate. Cut the curves with a saber saw or coping saw. Purchase a sheet of 3-inch-thick foam rubber that's the same size as your headboard. Use fabric glue to attach the foam rubber to the headboard. With an electric knife, cut the foam rubber to fit the curved corners.

3 ADD 10 inches to the dimensions of the headboard, and cut your rug fragment to these measurements. (Fabric should be turned so the woven edges run horizontally. With fabric that is 54 inches wide, you'll have a margin at the top of the headboard to turn to the back and tack in place. The lower edge can hang straight and not turn to the back.) Arrange the rug fragment facedown on the floor, and place the headboard, foam side down, on top. Pull the fabric to the back and staple. At the curves, arrange fabric in several neat folds, turn them to the back, and staple. Cut 54-inch-wide muslin 4 inches longer than the width of the headboard. Center muslin on back of headboard, turn extra fabric under, and staple in place. Lean headboard against wall, and pull bedframe up to headboard.

step 1

step 3

Getting Started

TOOLS & MATERIALS

- 1 (4- x 8-foot) sheet of 1-inch plywood
- saw
- yardstick
- hammer
- nails
- 2 (48-inch-long) 1 x 4s
- dinner plate
- saber saw or coping saw
- 1 (3-inch-thick) sheet of foam rubber
- fabric glue
- electric knife
- large rug fragment or fabric with design that can be positioned with the woven edges running horizontally
- scissors
- staple gun and staples
- muslin

TRANSFORMED *into* TERRA-COTTA

A simple paint finish turns a cast-concrete figure into something special. Paint one this afternoon.

Garden ornaments made of cast concrete are affordable, readily available, and you can use them as accents in both your house and garden. But they may look too new and too perfect when you first acquire them. You can soften their look by creating a weathered terra-cotta finish. It's easy to achieve this handsome patina by using everyday paint supplies. Latex paint and wood stain enable you to apply shading and highlights to simulate aging.

The finish is successful on statuary destined for interior or exterior use, but containers present complications from moisture. Try applying a concrete water sealant to a pot's interior. Or pack a large container with a layer of mulch, and line it with a plastic pot.

STEP-BY-STEP

1 PRIME the concrete figure by painting it off-white, beige, or light gray. Allow this coat to dry, then apply terra-cotta paint.

2 SHADE the entire piece by applying ebony wood stain or glazing liquid that's been tinted burnt umber. Rub away the shading with a rag, but let color remain in the crevices of the piece.

3 MIX a small amount of terra-cotta with some of the lighter paint. Retouch the statue by applying the lighter paint to raised areas. This will simulate bleaching by the sun. Refine the finish by continuing to add highlights and shadows.

Getting Started

TOOLS & MATERIALS

concrete statue

paintbrushes

off-white, beige, or light gray flat exterior latex paint (color used here: Bleached Bone by Martin Senour)

terra-cotta flat exterior latex paint (color used here: Serape by Martin Senour)

dark wood stain, such as Minwax Wood Finish in Ebony, or glazing liquid tinted burnt umber, such as Moore's Alkyd Glazing Liquid

rags

It didn't take long to give this concrete statue its weathered terra-cotta appearance. Painted shadows and highlights accentuate details of the figure's design.

EASY PROJECTS

MUDDY *COLORS*

Use drywall mud to create dimensional designs on accessories.

It's no surprise to read about creative methods of applying different kinds of paint through stencils, but drywall mud? The material that's used to fill dings and dents before walls are painted? Who would have thought that such imaginative effects would result from pressing this utilitarian material through a lacy stencil.

The technique is simple, and yet it yields wonderfully subtle patterns and textures. You'll need to purchase a stencil (or make one of your own by cutting designs into a sheet of Mylar). Place the stencil on a lampshade, box, frame, or other item, and use a putty knife to press the drywall mud through the openings. Lift the stencil, and repeat the design on other areas. Let the design dry; then paint and glaze the object with wood stain.

Getting Started

TOOLS & MATERIALS

- masking tape
- stencil
- box, frame, lampshade, or other object
- putty knife
- small container of drywall mud (or spackling compound)
- paintbrush
- acrylic craft paint
- sponge
- oil- or water-based wood stain
- rag or paper towel

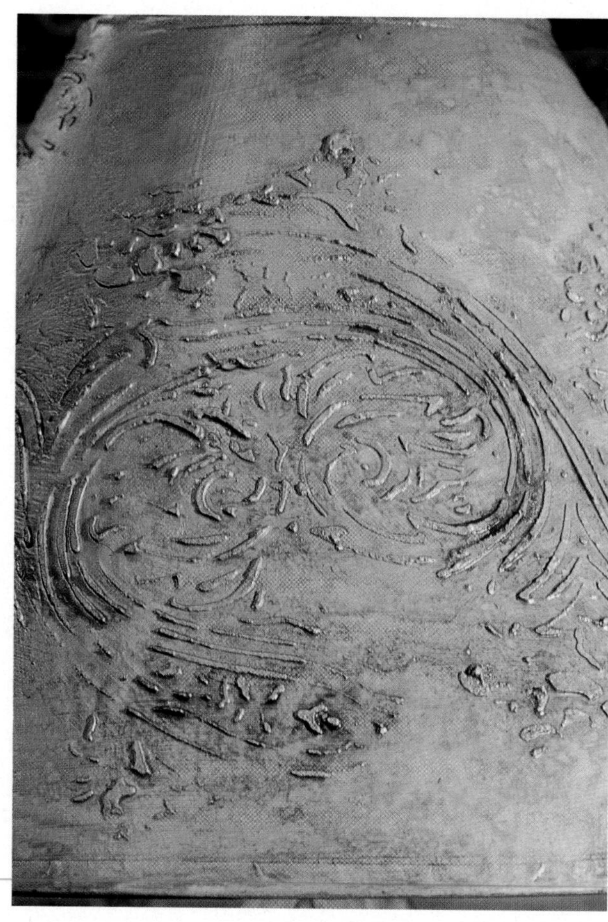

A plain paper lampshade gains textural charm with the addition of a raised pattern. Once the lampshade was painted, a dark wood stain was applied to accentuate the design.

A flat, wide picture frame provides an ideal surface for stenciling with drywall mud.

Small metal beads are nailed to the bottom of the wooden box as feet. An additional bead serves as a clasp.

STEP-BY-STEP

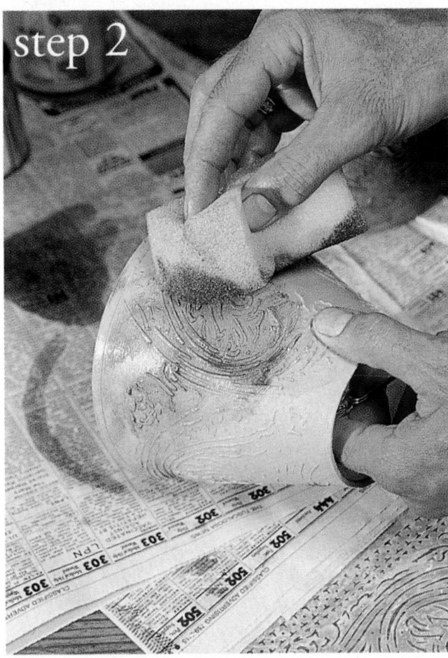

1 TAPE the stencil to the object you're decorating. Dip a putty knife into the drywall mud, and smooth the mud onto the stencil. Once the stencil is covered, remove it. Clean off the excess mud, and reposition the stencil. Continue applying the mud through the stencil until the surface is covered with the pattern. (After every two or three applications, rinse the drywall mud from the stencil to keep the openings from getting clogged.) Let the object dry completely.

2 PAINT the object with acrylic craft paint in the desired color. Let the paint dry. With a sponge, apply wood stain to the painted object. Use the sponge to create light and dark areas that accentuate the pattern.

3 CRUMPLE a rag or paper towel, and rub off some of the wood stain. Let the stain dry. Repeat steps, if desired, for additional texture and depth.

BEADED LAMPSHADES

Add glitz and glitter to plain paper shades with this quick idea.

Richly colored glass beads catch the light from these lamps in an intriguing way. By embellishing plain paper lampshades with glistening glass or metal beads, you can add a touch of individuality. The shades are perfect for chandeliers, table and floor lamps, or tiny lamps tucked into a bookshelf or open cabinet.

For this project you'll need beads, brass wire, and brass jump rings, which are used in jewelry-making.

getting STARTED

TOOLS & MATERIALS

- paper lampshades
- large needle
- small roll of 22-gauge brass wire
- ½-inch-diameter brass jump rings
- ⅜- and ¼-inch-diameter colored beads
- needle-nose pliers
- ¼-inch-diameter brass beads (found in the jewelry-making section of a crafts store)

STEP-BY-STEP

1 USE a large needle to pierce holes at ½-inch intervals near the edge of the lampshade. Cut a 30-inch-long piece of wire. Use ⅜-inch diameter beads in two colors.

2 PLACE the end of the wire through a hole, beginning on the inside of the shade. (Twist the last 2 inches of the wire so that it won't come through the first hole.) Place a bead on the wire.

3 THREAD the end of the wire through the next hole, again from the inside of the shade. Add a bead in the second color. Continue threading the wire through the holes and adding beads in alternating colors until you've gone all the way around the shade. On the inside of the shade, twist both ends of the wire securely together; then cut off excess.

Bead-trimmed lampshades add accents of rich color, instantly updating this pair of small brass lamps.

STEP-BY-STEP

1 PIERCE holes, using a large needle, at 1¼-inch intervals around the edge of a gold lampshade. Cut a 24-inch-long piece of wire. For the trim, use ½-inch-diameter brass jump rings, ⅜-inch-diameter and ¼-inch-diameter colored beads, as well as ¼-inch-diameter brass beads.

2 ALLOW one jump ring per hole. On each ring, place a brass bead between two ¼-inch-diameter colored beads. Insert the jump rings in the holes. Use the needle-nose pliers to open and close the jump rings.

3 THREAD the brass wire through one jump ring. (Twist the opposite end of the wire so that it won't pull through the jump ring.) Add one ⅜-inch-diameter colored bead; then thread the wire through the next jump ring and add a second bead. Continue threading the wire and adding beads until you've gone all the way around. Twist the ends of the wire together and cut off excess.

Getting Started

TOOLS & MATERIALS

54-inch-wide piece of velvet fabric in principal and accent colors

yardstick

pen

scissors

iron

⅞-inch-wide fusible fabric web (from fabric store)

lining fabric

straight pins

sewing machine

down pillow form or polyester fiberfill

needle and thread to match principal color of velvet

PERFECT HARMONY

Choose an array of velvets to create several soft-to-the-touch pillows.

Make these elegant accent pillows by weaving strips of two contrasting fabrics into squares. Then sew the squares to lining fabric, and attach the pillow backs. Fill each pillow cover with a soft pillow form.

Upholstery-weight velvet was used for these pillows, but dress-weight fabric would also be suitable. Select one or more colors already present in your room, and then consider adding one neutral shade, such as the taupe velvet used here.

While these pillows are lovely in a bedroom, they also make fine additions to deep sofas or daybeds. Or add one to your favorite armchair. You can even mix fabrics and still be assured of a well-coordinated look. For example, use leftover upholstery or slipcover fabric for one set of strips and the pillow back. Then choose a complementary shade of velvet for the other strips.

Or select a principal color for one set of strips and the pillow back, and choose an accent color for the remaining strips. Use fusible fabric web to secure raw edges and reduce the amount of sewing.

STEP-BY-STEP

1 MARK both colors of velvet into six 4-inch-wide strips that run from selvage (woven edge) to selvage. (This indicates lines for cutting fabric.) Mark fold lines 1 inch from cutting lines and outside edges of fabric. Cut the fabric into strips; then cut each strip into two 24-inch-long pieces. You'll need 11 strips each of the principal and accent colors.

2 FOLD 1 inch of fabric on long edges of each strip toward center. Iron the folds in place. Follow the manufacturer's instructions for applying the fusible fabric web under the folds.

3 CUT velvet pillow back (from principal color) and lining fabric, making each 24 inches square. Place square of lining fabric on table. At one corner, pin strip of fabric in principal color (right side up) to one edge of lining. Pin strip of accent color to adjoining edge. Continue pinning strips of each color in place, weaving them over and under to create a checkerboard pattern. Continue until all strips are woven together. Remove straight pins.

4 STITCH by machine, making a straight line ½ inch from edge of lining fabric. Place woven square and pillow back right sides together; machine-stitch 1 inch from edge of lining. Leave an 8-inch-long opening on one side. Clip excess fabric at corners and edges. Turn pillow cover right side out, and insert pillow form or polyester fiberfill. Stitch opening by hand.

YARDAGE AND CUTTING GUIDE

FABRIC REQUIREMENTS	22- x 22-inch pillow	18- x 18-inch pillow	14- x 14-inch pillow
principal color	1⅓ yards	1¼ yards	1 yard
accent color	⅔ yard	⅔ yard	½ yard
lining	⅔ yard	⅔ yard	⅔ yard
CUT THE FABRICS TO THE FOLLOWING DIMENSIONS:			
pillow back (cut from principal color)	24 x 24 inches	20 x 20 inches	16 x 16 inches
lining	24 x 24 inches	20 x 20 inches	16 x 16 inches
strips	Cut 6 strips 54" long; from these cut 11 strips 24" long.	Cut 5 strips 54" long; from these cut 9 strips 20" long.	Cut 3 strips 54" long; from these cut 7 strips 16" long.

step 2

step 3

Quick ACCENTS

Accessories add charm and personality to your home. In this section, you'll find suggestions for arranging favorite objects to create a dramatic tabletop display, simple steps for hanging pictures, and tips on styling your bookshelves.

QUICK ACCENTS

THE ART of DISPLAY

Give instant character to your tabletop with these terrific tips for combining accessories.

Every tabletop merits a tablescape, an arrangement that's composed of attractive and intriguing objects. With a little planning and experimentation, you'll find it easy to compose a tablescape that can remain in place for a long time without needing additional attention. Consider these suggestions when arranging your accessories.

STAGGER heights. Stack books to create an instant pedestal for a tureen or compote. Use a wooden stand to raise a small lamp. When a chest or table stands against a wall, try to include one object that extends to eye level; then place items at gradually decreasing heights to direct attention down to the tabletop.

UNITE with color. Choose accessories tinged with a common color, such as blue, rust, green, or gold. Or you can use another hue that complements your particular room. Fill out the arrangement with art and accessories in neutral shades.

VARY the textures. Unusual surface qualities, such as the crackle of handblown glass or the sheen of leather-bound books, provide visual interest. Place a rough basket beside a glass bottle; accentuate the surface of a rusty iron object by contrasting it with glazed porcelain.

INCLUDE the organic. The most appealing item in a room is often organic in origin. It may be a wonderful object constructed of wood, a simple bouquet of flowers, or a bowl of fresh fruit. For your tabletop, select a vase or other container that is attractive even when empty; then add flowers when available. Or choose a handsome cake stand; then bring in color with fruit or vegetables.

Combine objects made of organic materials, such as wood, paper, clay, and natural fibers. Place a round table against a wall to make an innovative side table.

Use color to unify a group of objects; most of these are tinged with blue. Framed photos lean casually against the wall.

Symmetrical placement of objects works well for this iron-and-glass coffee table, where the tablescape is designed to be viewed from all sides.

ACCENT with art. As a visual expression of an artist's thoughts, art enriches any setting. There's no need to hang every painting or print; a relaxed effect is achieved by leaning a frame against the wall. Handmade crafts, such as a wooden box or a nest of bowls, will also convey originality.

BALANCE the design. Symmetrical balance is achieved when half of a tabletop arrangement is roughly a mirror image of the other half. Set a significant accessory in the center; place objects to each side that are similar in size and shape.

PERSONALIZE it. Let your tablescape refer to your family, travels, or experiences. Include a photograph or souvenir as a reminder of a favorite trip. Add a keepsake that reminds you of its donor.

LIGHTEN the mood. When appropriate, add a touch of whimsy. There's much humor to be found in miniature versions of familiar objects. Do you love the sun and sand? Display a tiny beach chair. Or if you own a small wooden stool, use it to elevate another object.

REFER to the past. Antiques and old objects often possess a rich patina. Include something from times past, perhaps from another culture, in your tablescape.

KEEP it current. Bring your display up-to-the-moment by including an object from the present. A campaign button, a restaurant menu, or books of popular fiction will provide this link.

QUICK ACCENTS

One can be a lonely number when you're hanging a single picture. Think multiples. After all, there's...

STRENGTH IN NUMBERS

In many instances, if one is good, two or more is better. This truism applies to second helpings, movie double features, and, yes, hanging pictures. Here are a few lessons you'll want to complete. Let us give you a hint—the correct answers are multiple choices.

PICTURE HANGING HOW-TOS

1 MARK and measure the upper left and right corners of the area where you'll be hanging your pictures. Use a ruler or measuring tape to make sure the ends are level. Using pushpins at each end, tie a string to mark this imaginary line.

2 ALWAYS hang your two outside pictures first. Hang frames so the tops touch the string of your imaginary line. Make sure the sides line up and the frames are straight. As a general rule of thumb, the distance between frames should equal the size of the mat in your picture or print.

3 WHEN hanging an odd number of identical frames, hang the center one next. Measure the distance between the two outer frames and mark the center point. From this point hang the third picture. Again, make sure the top of the frame touches the string.

When hanging an even number of identical frames, start by measuring the distance between the two outer frames, and mark the center point. Then measure the total width of all the remaining frames. Subtract this measurement from the distance between the two outer frames. This will give you the distance between each frame; divide the distance by 2. Mark this measurement on either side of the center mark, and hang the two middle frames at these points.

(RIGHT) **It may look like seven individual frames, but look again. The big brass frame beautifully pulls together several small paintings. The eggplant mat background unifies the artwork into one cohesive image. The brass portrait light picks up the subtle colors in each picture.**

Be sure to hang an oversize frame from heavy bolts that are suitable for your type of wall.

(ABOVE) **Set at eye level for guests seated around the table, four botanical prints extend along the chair rail. Use simple frames with clean, bold lines. Fussy frames just won't add up here.**

(RIGHT) **The vegetable print grouping highlights this breakfast room's garden theme. Three smaller prints rest comfortably above three larger prints.**

(LEFT) **With careful placement, four pictures make one wonderful statement, as these Audubon prints illustrate. Notice how the white space of each mat matches the amount of space between frames.**

tip Dry mount inexpensive prints that are to be displayed in rooms subject to heat and humidity. It will prevent them from curling and ripping.

With similar colors, composition, and media, these two paintings make perfect companions. Distinctive frames add interest and texture. Hung alone, each painting would be too small in relation to the sturdy étagère below. Twin urns resting on ornamental brackets complement the paintings and add balance to the display.

QUICK ACCENTS

Interesting HANG-UPS

So you may not have yet found the ideal painting or print. Don't worry. Just use your imagination.

If the perfect piece of artwork eludes you, consider several creative alternatives. Some of the most fascinating ornaments wait in unexpected places. Rummage through salvage yards and secondhand stores to find objects with strong outlines or silhouettes that you can hang over a bed or feature above a fireplace or sofa. Explore flea markets and junk shops to find a time-worn window frame or some other worthy architectural element. Let the equipment from a favorite sport—polo mallets, golf clubs, fishing poles—add an athletic element to a room's decor. Just about anything's fair game if you like the object and won't grow weary of seeing it every day.

Mount the selected items securely with appropriate bolts or hangers. (The local hardware store can help you choose the best ones.) You may want to add some form of accent lighting to get the best effect.

Old pieces often have finishes that are less than perfect, but most surface flaws only contribute to the overall charm. The weathered look of reclaimed metal, worn wood, and peeling paint will add a sense of timelessness and a patina of age to your home. And guests will toast your creativity as they consider the treasures awaiting in their own garages and attics.

Fabric in a morning glory design dresses the windows and bed. A curvy fragment from an old garden gate stands in for a headboard and accentuates the room's delightful botanical style.

With prized fish trophies displayed over the bed, this room features an outdoors theme. Fishing paraphernalia (including a collection of old rods and lures), wicker pieces, and plaid fabrics accent the room's comfortably casual look.

(RIGHT) **Dark wood and brass accents bring a masculine feel to this boy's bedroom. Crossed polo mallets animate the wallspace above the sleigh bed.**

QUICK ACCENTS

TRAYS *for* DISPLAY

Use trays for backing a bookcase, fashioning a table, or embellishing a wall.

You can quickly add character to a bookshelf, wall, or tabletop by using a tray as a decorative accessory. First, explore the possibilities among those you've previously used for serving. You can find handsome trays in antiques stores; secondhand shops and garage sales are also good sources. Don't shy away from worn or darkened pieces; their weathered finish will complement old objects you already own. To find new trays that are quite affordable, look through gift catalogs and check imports shops as well as furniture and department stores.

SHELF LIFE

By leaning trays against the back of a bookcase or setting them in plate stands, you can form an unusual and varied background for other objects. This display idea is especially useful with an expanse of built-in shelving. You can create depth by layering small objects in related colors along the shelves and mixing in items made of contrasting materials. Add some framed prints, paintings, boxes, books, tiles, and brackets for greater interest and individuality.

DECK THE WALLS

A vertical grouping of trays in various sizes makes an innovative accent for a breakfast room, kitchen, or dining room. Because the largest in the group will usually look the heaviest, it should be placed lowest in the arrangement.

Wire hangers sized for trays are usually available in hardware stores and accessory shops. Look for hangers with plastic-coated tips that won't damage the tray's finish. Plan the position of each tray before driving a nail. First, arrange all the items on the floor, or tape pieces of paper to the wall to find the best configuration. Then use a yardstick and pencil to measure and mark the correct positions on the wall. Use a picture hanger for support, or a bolt inserted in a wall stud.

A collection of old black tole (hand-painted tinware) trays provides a dark and dramatic counterpoint to the shelves' pastel green wall color. Additions of pots, books, art, and fruit play on the light-dark contrast. When small trays are set upright, it's easy to appreciate their hand-painted designs.

WOLFMAN • GOLD
FORKS, KNIVES & SPOONS
Antiques At Home
JOHN LORING

TABLE MATTERS

The idea of forming a table by setting a portable tray onto a base dates at least to the eighteenth century, and it makes as much sense now as it did then. In furniture stores you'll see mahogany and cherry reproduction tray tables that are appropriate for formal rooms; antiques shops are excellent sources for old trays set into custom-made wooden bases.

It's easy to improvise a coffee table by setting an ottoman in front of a sofa, and then topping it with a large gallery tray. You can readily fashion an end table from a tray and a variety of bases, such as a folding luggage rack or a portable camp stool. Beside a chair, arrange a 15- to 18-inch-tall stack of books and top it off with a tray.

An antique tray set on a faux bamboo stand makes an elegant accent for a formal living room. The tasseled footstool fills open space beneath the graceful table. The lustrous black surface is embellished with gold detailing and mother-of-pearl inlay.

OTHER TRICKS WITH TRAYS

- COVER your open fireplace for the summer by positioning a large tray between the andirons and grate. It will offer pattern and color when seen through the fire screen.
- ORGANIZE a tabletop grouping of small treasures. Place an ornamental tray on a table, and fill the tray with assorted boxes, porcelains, or favorite framed photographs.
- FEATURE an urn or vase by placing it against a tall tray that's a contrasting color. Lean the tray against the wall, and place a container of plants, twigs, or flowers in front.
- ADD height to a tall chest or an armoire by hanging a tray above it. A distinctive tray mounted on the wall or set on a stand is an excellent way to fill wallspace, especially in a room with a high ceiling.
- UNDERSCORE a leggy table by placing a large tray underneath it; you can put the tray on a stand or stabilize it by stacking a few books in front. Fill out the arrangement with wicker baskets or ceramic jars; add a plant (such as a Chinese evergreen) that doesn't require much light.
- DISGUISE unsightly switches and electrical outlets along your kitchen's backsplash with trays that repeat some of the room's colors. As a bonus, the trays will be handy for serving.
- PLACE a favorite tray in the center of your dining table, and add a tall plant, vase of flowers, or piece of garden statuary. Supplement with pots of ferns or trailing ivy. Cluster pieces of fresh fruit on the tray for added color.
- COLLECT simple wooden, tin, or bamboo trays to use instead of place mats. Guests will also enjoy using them at your next dinner party.

QUICK ACCENTS

SHELVES *with* STYLE

Let your bookshelves provide a stage for displaying art, collections, and personal mementos.

A bookcase is a three-dimensional scrapbook with shelves instead of pages. Fill it with memories—rich photos, favorite books, and the "must have" souvenir brought back from vacation.

LIGHT & BRIGHT

With an eye for symmetry, these bookshelves (left and below) are arranged around a blue-and-white porcelain collection. Here are five ideas we used:

1 If you have adjustable bookshelves, place them at different heights. The center unit has four shelves, and the outer units have five, each maintaining symmetry.

2 Take a page from English Country style. Hang a favorite painting on the front of your shelves. Solid books make a wonderful background for this look. Two paintings balance each other, reflecting the classic style.

3 Group small objects, such as family photos, together. Place tall objects behind them to serve as a visual anchor.

4 Line the insides of your shelves with a subtle wallpaper, such as this narrow yellow stripe.

5 Use a deep shelf as a desk area to hold stationery or correspondence.

Groups of antique books are carefully interspersed with objects of varying shape and size, giving the shelves a balanced look.

RICH & WARM

A collection of antique books is a wonderful starting point for styling bookshelves (above). Open up a chapter from these organizational ideas.

1 Paint the back of your bookshelves. Here royal red serves as an elegant backdrop to the antique books and unifies the overall look.

2 When possible, remove one shelf to create a tall display space for showcasing a favorite painting or other large object.

3 Use larger books stacked on their sides as pedestals for picture frames, small ceramics, or tiny boxes.

4 Gold accents work well against this warm red background. A gold wooden dragonfly and ceramic Granny Smith apples add unexpected interest and shapes.

TOP-SHELF TIPS

- DISPLAY your favorite personal items—they will tell a story about you to friends and family.
- KEEP in mind shelf heights should barely clear the largest object to make the shelves appear full.
- CHOOSE low-light houseplants in interesting containers to add texture and color.
- DISPLAY a favorite book or one with a pretty cover against the back wall.
- ADD a bowl of fresh fruit or a vase of cut flowers when guests are visiting.
- REARRANGE periodically, adding new treasures.

DECORATING *details*

These cheery ideas will add touches of color and fun without a lot of effort.

THE GRASS IS GREENER INSIDE Bring a bit of summer indoors. Plant ryegrass seed in attractive pots; in a few short days you'll see sprouts coming up. Give the grass a haircut when it gets too long and scraggly.

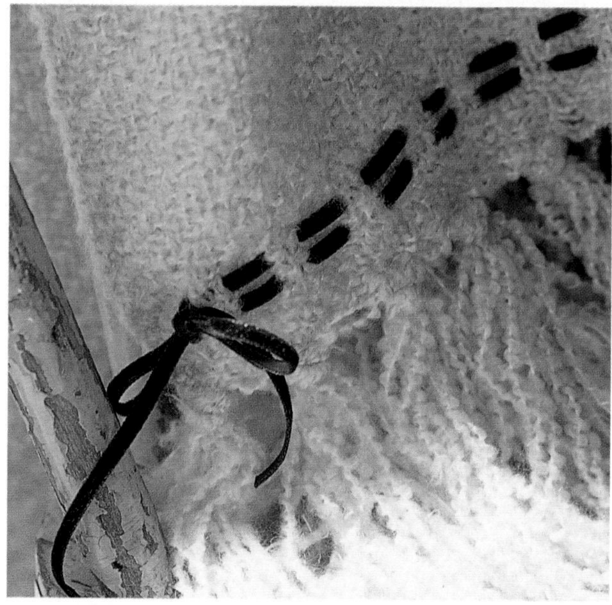

WEAVING DETAIL Trim a blanket with velvet ribbon for a touch of warmth. Using a craft needle or large safety pin, weave ribbon through a loose-woven blanket. Finish by tying the ends of the ribbon into a bow.

PLACE MAT PIZZAZZ **Perk up your tabletop by attaching two rows of ribbon or one stripe of rickrack along the short ends of place mats. Or fold wide ribbon over the edge to create a panel. Sew a border all the way around for a framed effect.**

(ABOVE) NATURAL HEADBOARD Cut lengths of grapevine from your garden or purchase several wreaths from a crafts-supply store, and arrange them on the wall for a natural headboard. You could also connect the wreaths with florist wire to create a layered effect, and then hang them on the wall with a nail.

(LEFT) FABULOUS FABRIC ART Display your favorite fabric swatches in simple painted frames on any tabletop. Purchase a wooden frame, discard the glass, and paint the frame with acrylic craft paint to match the fabric you will use. Let it dry thoroughly. Trim the swatch and a piece of cardboard to fit inside the frame. Attach the fabric to the cardboard with double-sided tape along the edges, and place in the frame. Arrange in a grouping of complementary fabrics.

BOWL OF BALLS Round out a shelf or tabletop with decorative balls. Try these do-it-yourself ones made from plastic foam. Choose several shades of the same color of tissue to give depth. Mix white craft glue and water to make a soupy consistency. Cut the tissue in small pieces; dip them in the glue mixture. Apply the wet tissue to the ball. Continue until the ball is covered.

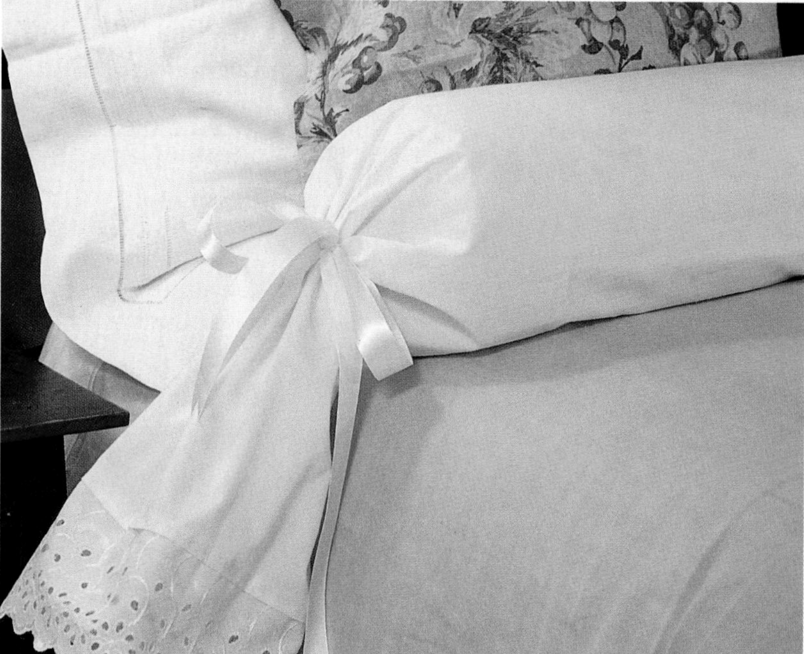

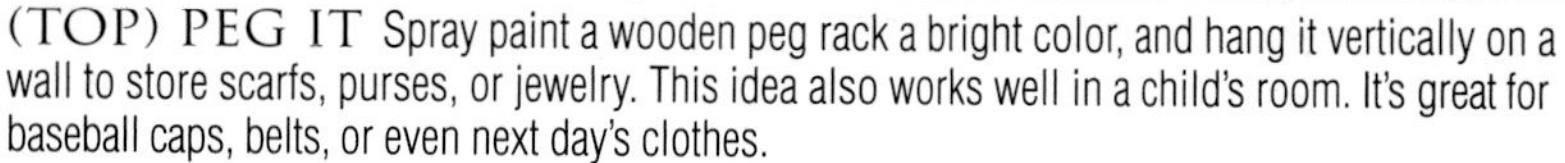

(TOP) PEG IT Spray paint a wooden peg rack a bright color, and hang it vertically on a wall to store scarfs, purses, or jewelry. This idea also works well in a child's room. It's great for baseball caps, belts, or even next day's clothes.

QUICK BOLSTER Enhance your bed linens with a decorative pillow easily made from a king-size case and ribbon. Purchase a bolster pillow form from an upholstery fabric store. Simply insert the bolster form into the pillowcase, and tie in place with a complementary ribbon. You can easily change the color to match your decor. Make several bolsters to add a sense of luxury to your bed.

FESTIVE BOTTLE TOPPERS Crown distinctive bottles with these fun-to-make cork stoppers. Use craft paint or paint pens to decorate wooden knobs with whimsical swirls and polka dots; finish with a coat of clear varnish. String beads on copper or stainless steel wire, and attach wire to the knob by drilling a small hole in top of knob. Secure it with silicone adhesive and sealer. Drill a hole through the cork and knob, connecting the two with a dowel screw (threaded on both ends) and silicone adhesive and sealer. Tip: Take your bottle with you to the hardware store to choose the correct-size cork.

THROW IN THE TOWEL
Sew simple pillows from kitchen towels. Seam short ends together to create a tube. On the open ends, make six buttonholes—three on each side—and attach buttons to match up with holes. Insert a pillow form (we used a 14- x 18-inch form), and button ends together.

Weekend WORKSHOP

A weekend is all you need to master the possibilities in this chapter. Saw a shelf, construct a cabinet, or craft an instant antique. All the help you need is included on the following pages.

SHELF LIFE

Add display space to any room, using a wooden shelf constructed from the enclosed patterns.

Painted shelves provide an attractive way of featuring your favorite collectibles and framed photographs. Making the shelves requires only handtools; but you can more easily make the angled cuts with a band saw or jigsaw, if one is available.

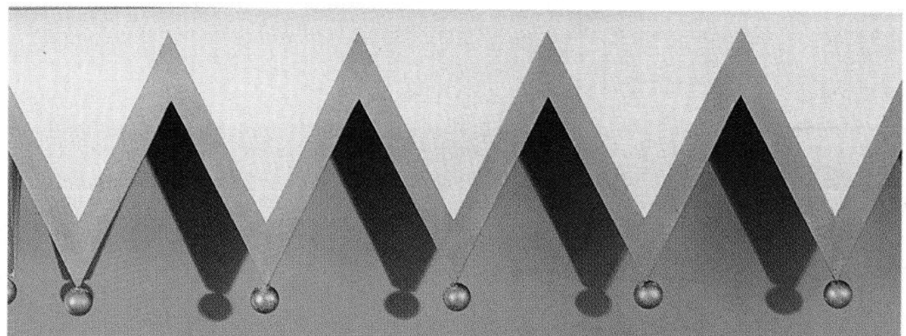

The front and side pieces of the shelf are made from the full width of a 1 x 8 (about 7½ inches). Equipped with a handsaw, backsaw, and miter box, you can cut the front and sides at home, using the patterns on pages 142-144.

The top for one small shelf measures 6 x 17 inches. This means that you must cut a 1½-inch strip from the length of the board. Try to have this piece cut at a lumberyard or cabinet shop because it's difficult to rip the board (cut along its length) with a handsaw.

Assemble the shelf, and glue wooden beads to the points; then use paint to jazz it up in a creative and personal way.

getting STARTED

TOOLS & MATERIALS

- pencil
- tissue paper or tracing paper
- carbon paper
- ruler
- 1 (8-foot) piece of 1 x 8 for 2 (17-inch-wide) shelves (select a soft wood, such as spruce, poplar, pine, or cedar)
- handsaw
- sandpaper
- miter box and backsaw
- wood glue
- finishing nails
- nail set
- hammer
- wood putty
- ¾-inch wooden beads (optional)
- 1½-inch nails that will fit holes in beads
- drill
- latex primer
- paintbrush
- latex paint, satin finish
- roll of ¾-inch masking tape
- scissors or craft knife
- acrylic paint for borders
- oil paint pens
- 2 (2-inch) inside corner braces per shelf
- carpenter's level
- screws
- screwdriver

tip Stack 2 or 3 small shelves on a narrow wallspace. Paint them the color of your room's wooden trim.

(ABOVE) **You can build a shelf that's double, even triple, the length of the shorter one. Simply trace the following pattern two or three times onto a board that's proportionately longer. You can cut the wood by hand or use a jigsaw. Add detail by attaching a wooden bead to each point.**

(RIGHT) **Individualize your shelves with painted borders that are color-keyed to your walls and accessories. Add touches of pattern with oil paint pens.**

FRONT OF SHELF, LEFT

FRONT OF SHELF, RIGHT

SIDE OF SHELF

1 TRACE the patterns (pages 142-144) onto tissue paper or tracing paper. Use carbon paper to transfer the traced designs to wood. Straighten lines with ruler.

2 CUT one piece of wood by the pattern on pages 142-143; cut two according to the pattern on page 144. Sand all edges of each piece.

3 MITER the corners by following these steps: Place the front of the shelf in the miter box. Make 45-degree cuts at the left and right edges; then place each side piece in the miter box, and cut the front edge of each one to 45 degrees.

4 USE wood glue and small finishing nails to join the sides to the front. To make the shelf top, cut a 17-inch length of the 1 x 8. Cut along the length of the piece to rip it to 6 inches in width. (Reminder: This cut is easier with a table saw; a lumberyard or cabinet shop may be able to do this for you.) Sand all edges. Join the top to the front and sides using wood glue and finishing nails. Place a nail set (metal tool shaped like a pencil) on each nailhead; use a hammer to tap the nail set lightly, countersinking each nail. Fill holes with wood putty; then sand smooth.

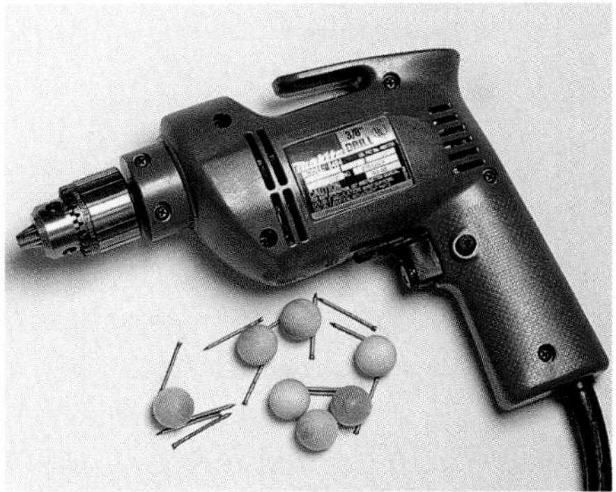

5 (optional) ATTACH wooden beads by first drilling a hole in each point of the shelf; then insert a nail into each bead. Apply glue to pointed tip of nails, and insert one in every hole in shelf.

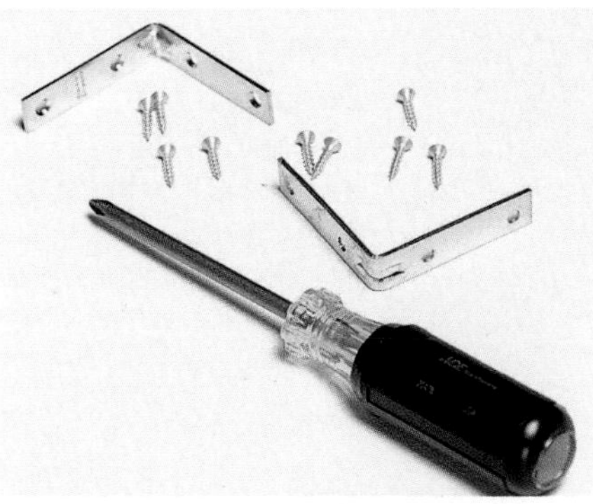

7 ATTACH inside corner braces to wall, positioning one over a wall stud, if possible. Use a carpenter's level to get shelf straight. Place shelf temporarily on inside corner braces. Mark screw holes on underside of shelf top. Remove shelf, and drill pilot holes. Replace shelf on inside corner braces, aligning holes with pilot holes. Insert screws.

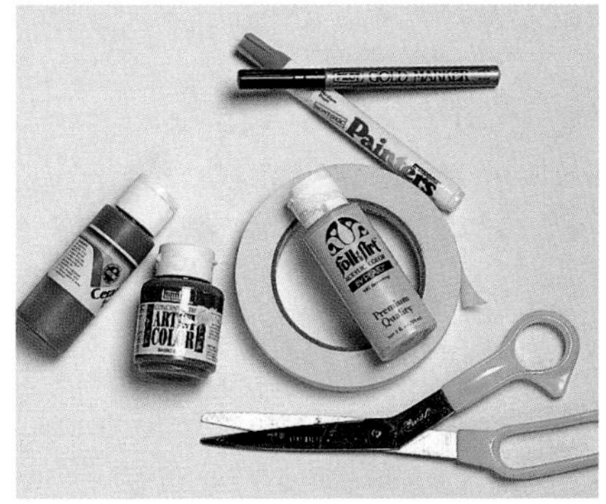

6 GIVE the shelf a coat of latex primer, and sand. Paint the shelf in your choice of colors. Use $\frac{3}{4}$-inch masking tape as a guide in painting neat borders both on points and on top of shelf. Apply a row of tape along the edge of each point. Use scissors or a craft knife to make angled cuts; then place a second row of tape beside the first. Remove the first row of tape. Smooth down edges of remaining tape. Apply acrylic paint to surface between tape and edges of wood. Paint bottom edges of points and beads, if used. Remove tape. Paint edges of shelf top. Use oil paint pens to add details, if desired.

W E E K E N D   W O R K S H O P

Screen Play

Not a carpenter? Not a painter?
You can still make this fashionable folding screen.

Building a screen is an enjoyable project that you can easily accomplish. This playful piece enables you to divide space in a room while giving you five panels on which to display small prints and other decorative elements. It is 5 feet 11 inches high (including the balls at top) and is about 36 inches wide when standing. Ideal for a dressing area or girl's room, it can organize a whole wardrobe of hair ribbons and necklaces. And you can stain or paint it in any combination of colors.

Built from pieces of nominal 1- x 10-inch pine (actual size ¾ x 9¼ inches) and accented with wooden drawer pulls, this screen is stained white and gray; the light finish lets the wood grain show through. The knobs are left unfinished to accent the wood's natural color. A saber saw and a sander will make it easier for you to achieve the crisp, carefully finished appearance of this example.

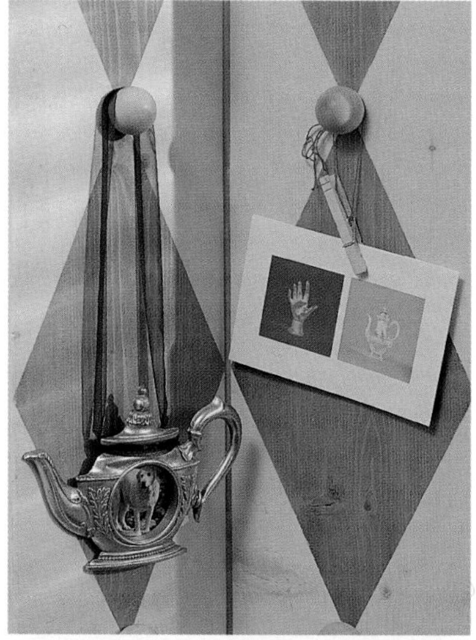

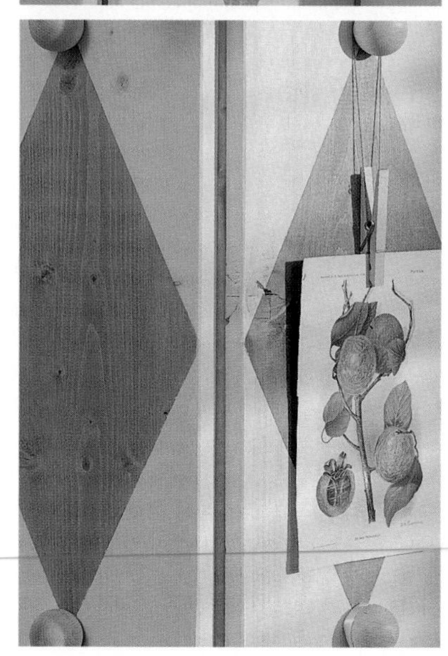

TOOLS & MATERIALS

- saber saw or handsaw
- 5 (8-foot-long) pieces of 1- x 10-inch pine
- pencil
- yardstick
- sandpaper or electric sander
- tack cloth
- masking tape
- paintbrushes
- gray wood stain
- white wood stain
- satin-finish polyurethane
- drill and drill bits
- 5 hanger bolts to fit
- 5 (2-inch-diameter) unfinished wooden ball knobs
- 15 (1½-inch-diameter) unfinished wooden ball knobs with screws
- 8 hinges with wood screws

A five-panel screen painted gray and white adds a touch of contemporary elegance wherever you place it. The knobs are useful for hanging items from ribbon, thread, or cording.

STEP-BY-STEP

1 CUT each piece of wood to 5 feet 9 inches in length. With a pencil and yardstick, mark the diamond design on each piece, using the sketch (at right) as a guide. Cut the point at the top of the screen. Sand all surfaces and edges, and remove all sanding dust with a tack cloth.

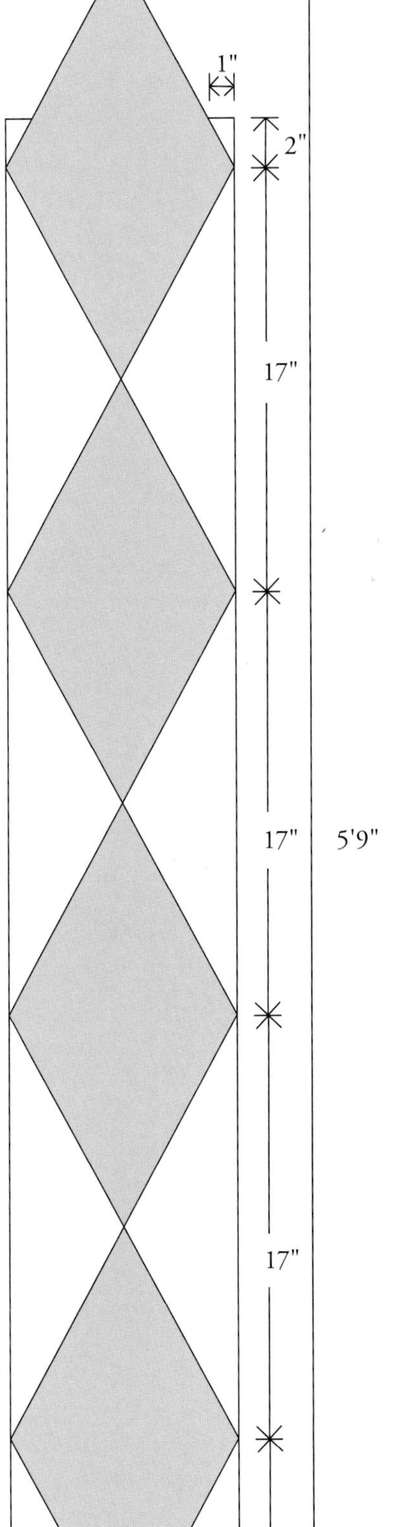

2 OUTLINE the gray diamonds with masking tape. Carefully smooth down the edge of the masking tape.

3 BRUSH gray stain into the outlined diamonds; let dry, and remove tape. Repeat step 2, only this time outline the outside areas with tape and apply white stain. Let dry, and remove tape. Apply white stain to the edges and back of all screen panels. Seal all surfaces with a coat of polyurethane.

4 DRILL pilot holes for hanger bolts in the points at the top of each screen panel. Screw hanger bolts into holes, and screw larger wooden knobs onto them. At points where gray diamonds meet, drill holes for screws. Insert screws through back of screen, and attach smaller wooden knobs to front. Mark positions of hinges. (Top of bottom hinge should be approximately 8½ inches from bottom edge of panel. Top hinge should be positioned at same distance from top.) Drill pilot holes. Place hinges on screen, and insert screws.

WEEKEND WORKSHOP

Make a *Shutter Cabinet*

Finished in periwinkle with white undertones, this shutter cabinet makes a nice addition to the kitchen, and it's perfect for storing canned goods.

Crafted from plywood shelving and two interior shutters, this cabinet is a handsome addition to any kitchen or bathroom. First, assemble the shelf body; then attach the shutters with hinges. The piece is finished with an easy two-toned, distressed paint technique. Decorative silver pulls add the final touch.

All the materials can be purchased at your local building-supply store. However, you may want to shop at a home-decorating store for special pulls. The project does require knowledge of basic woodworking and access to a few power tools. So read the instructions thoroughly before you buy materials or begin construction. For safety and accuracy, think through each step before doing it. Be sure to double-check every dimension before cutting. Wear eye and ear protection. And please read and follow the warnings and operating instructions that came with your tools.

STEP-BY-STEP

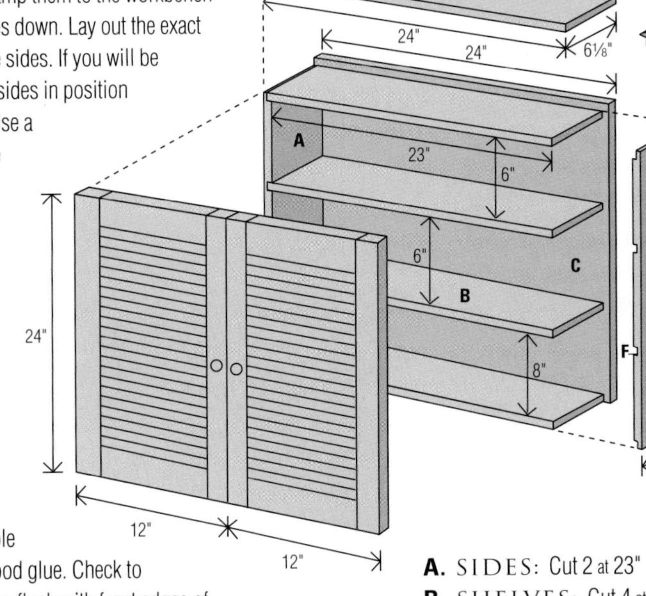

1 CUT the two sides (from the 1 x 6 shelving boards) to exact size. Clamp them to the workbench side by side, with outside faces down. Lay out the exact locations of the dadoes on the sides. If you will be routing the dadoes, leave the sides in position and rout both sides at once. Use a long straightedge to guide the router. You can also cut the dadoes in a similar manner using a portable circular saw fitted with a dado blade. Or you can cut the dadoes, one side at a time, on a table saw or radial arm saw. Next, cut the four shelves (from the 1 x 6 shelving boards) to size. Then sand the inside of both sides and the top and bottom of each shelf. Assemble the shelves and sides with wood glue. Check to make sure fronts of shelves are flush with front edges of sides; make sure that assembly is square, and leave to dry.

A. SIDES: Cut 2 at 23" x 5½"
B. SHELVES: Cut 4 at 23" x 5½"
C. BACK: Cut 1 at 23" x 24"
D. HEADER: Cut 1 at 24" x 6⅛"
E. MOLDING: Cut 1 at 25⅛" and 2 at 6¾"
F. DADOES: 5/16" x ¼"

2 CUT plywood back to 23 x 24 inches. Drill 2¼-inch holes for hanging. Drill the holes 3 inches from the top and 4 inches from the sides. Sand the good face, and glue to the back. Secure with finishing nails.

step 4

3 CUT the header board (from the 1 x 8 shelving board); then sand sides and top. Attach to the top of the cabinet with back side flush to back of cabinet. The front side should overhang. With a miter box, cut one piece of molding measuring 25⅛ inches and two pieces measuring 6¾ inches. Glue the long piece to the front of the header board and a smaller piece to either side. Secure with finishing nails.

4 BEGIN painting by first sanding with a fine-medium grade sanding sponge to smooth edges. Clean dust using a tack cloth. With a sponge brush, apply the base color using latex paint thinned with water (two parts paint to one part water). Apply a second coat. Coverage does not have to be even. Let dry; sand lightly. Paint two coats of the top color with the same formula as before.

5 REMOVE topcoat with a sanding sponge in areas that would be naturally worn. Follow the grain of the wood. Sand the top color, revealing the under color. (It's fine to sometimes reveal bare wood). Wipe free of debris.

6 APPLY an umber-tinted paste wax with a clean, soft cotton cloth. Work in small areas following the grain, and buff to desired luster.

7 DRILL holes for pulls. Position shutters on cabinet while it's lying down, and mark placement of the catches. (They would be best positioned at second shelf.) Follow manufacturer's instructions to attach hardware. Next, mark where hinges should attach. Drill small holes in marked areas; screw hinges in place, attaching doors. Attach pulls, and then hang shelf on wall with bolts.

Getting Started

TOOLS & MATERIALS

2 (8-foot-long) 1- x 6-inch shelving boards (pine, birch, or plywood)

portable circular saw

clamps

fine-medium grade sandpaper and sanding sponge

wood glue

2- x 2-foot piece of ¼-inch plywood

drill

1¼-inch finishing nails

hammer

1 (2-foot-long) 1- x 8-inch shelving board (pine, birch, or plywood)

miter box and miter saw

4 feet of cove molding

tack cloth

sponge brushes

two colors of latex paint

umber-tinted paste wax

cotton cloth

decorative pulls

pencil

2 (12- x 24-inch) shutters

2 double roller catches

4 (1- x ½-inch) butt hinges

toggle bolts

CRAFTED MIRROR

Create an instant focal point and add the illusion of space with this handsome do-it-yourself mirror.

Whenever you need to create the effect of bigger and brighter space in a room, you can always rely on the magic of a mirror. One classic and decorative mirror style, the trumeau (pronounced TRUE-mo), consists of a wide frame that incorporates a decorative element or a painting. The intricate moldings and hand-applied detailing give it a degree of formality. Antiques shops and home-furnishing stores are good sources of trumeau-style mirrors, or construct your own using these instructions.

STEP-BY-STEP

1 CUT plywood panel to 20 x 36 inches. From center of panel, cut out a rectangle measuring 23¾ x 13¾ inches, leaving approximately 9 inches of wood at top of panel, 3 inches at each side, and 3 inches at bottom.

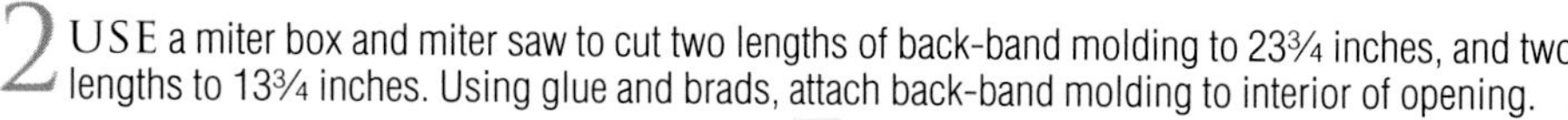

2 USE a miter box and miter saw to cut two lengths of back-band molding to 23¾ inches, and two lengths to 13¾ inches. Using glue and brads, attach back-band molding to interior of opening.

3 USE miter box and miter saw to cut two lengths of base molding to 36 inches and two lengths to 20 inches. Attach base molding with glue and brads to outer face of panel.

4 USE miter box to cut two lengths of lattice (on narrow edge) to 20½ inches and two lengths to 36½ inches. Attach lattice with glue and brads to outer edge of panel, ensuring that lattice is flush with back surface of panel.

5 COUNTERSINK all brad heads with nail set/punch; fill with putty. Lightly sand surfaces. Clean with tack cloth.

6 APPLY two coats of terra-cotta paint to wood appliqué and surfaces of frame. Paint plywood (not moldings or appliqué) with crackle medium; let dry.

7 COVER moldings with tape. Paint surface of plywood with one coat of flat ivory latex paint, working quickly with minimal brushstrokes. Allow to dry. Apply one coat of clear sealer. Let dry.

8 MASK crackled areas with tape; apply gold-leaf paint to all moldings and appliqué. Allow to dry. Attach appliqué with glue. Remove tape, and lightly sand gold-leaf surface to expose terra-cotta base coat. Wipe with tack cloth.

9 BRUSH tinted burnt umber glaze onto all surfaces; let dry. Take frame to glass company to install mirror, back the frame with paper or cardboard, and attach appropriate hangers and wire.

Measuring approximately 21 x 36 inches, our version of the trumeau is easy to build from plywood and stock molding. The ribbon motif is made of pressed wood. A crackled paint finish adds to the aged look. Once the frame was completed, it was fitted with a beveled mirror.

Getting Started

TOOLS & MATERIALS

- saber saw
- handsaw
- tape measure
- 2- x 4-foot piece of ½-inch birch plywood
- miter box and miter saw
- 8 feet of 11⁄16- x ½-inch back-band molding with stop
- wood glue
- 1-inch wire brads
- 12 feet of 1- x 1½-inch base molding
- 12 feet of lattice
- nail set/punch
- wood putty
- fine sandpaper
- tack cloth
- paintbrushes
- terra-cotta latex paint, eggshell finish
- decorative wood appliqué, 14 x 5½ inches
- crackle medium
- painter's tape (a type of low-adhesive masking tape)
- ivory latex paint, flat finish
- water-based clear sealer
- gold-leaf paint
- glazing medium, tinted burnt umber
- 23- x 13-inch piece of mirrored glass (optional: ¾-inch bevel)
- paper or cardboard
- mirror hangers
- wire

CRAFT an instant ANTIQUE

Readymade furniture legs, finials, and wood trim make it easy to assemble a table that looks hand carved.

Visit a well-stocked lumberyard or home-building center, and you may be pleasantly surprised at the variety of materials you'll find to use in building furniture.

This table is constructed of stock unfinished parts—legs, finials, and wood appliqués (sculptural cutouts made of pressed wood). To make the table taller, fencepost finials are attached to the bottom of the French-style legs.

The remaining parts of the table—the top and apron (the horizontal boards beneath the tabletop)—are cut from pine 1 x 8s.

Once you've become aware of the type of furniture legs, finials, and wood appliqués that are available in your area, you may need to modify the dimensions of the table. Select the wood appliqués first to ensure that the apron is the correct size.

step 1

step 2

step 3

step 4

STEP-BY-STEP

1 CUT wood into dimensions noted under Getting Started. Join one long piece (the front of the apron) to the top of the two legs, using wood glue and three corner braces at each joint. (Note: A pipe clamp is used to keep the wood stationary until the glue dries.) Repeat this step, joining the back of the apron to the top of the other two legs. Then attach the short pieces (the sides) to the front and back pieces.

2 DRILL a pilot hole at the bottom of each table leg, and screw a fencepost finial into the end.

3 CONSTRUCT the tabletop, using wood glue to join the three 38¾-inch-long pieces of wood. (Place the wider piece of wood in the center.) With the tabletop wrong side up, space five mending plates along the length of each joint. Secure with ½-inch wood screws. Use pipe clamps to hold the tabletop together until the glue dries.

Place the tabletop face down, and center the table/apron assembly on top of it, upside down. On all four sides, use 1-inch corner braces placed at 6-inch intervals to attach the tabletop to the apron. Sand the table. Use wood glue to attach appliqués to the apron. Be careful not to get glue on exposed surfaces.

4 APPLY two coats of white wood stain to the base of the table, following instructions on the can of stain. (A circular artist's brush is helpful for painting the appliqués.) With a sponge brush, apply a light coat of white stain to one board of the tabletop, following the grain of the wood; immediately wipe the stain away, using a soft rag. Repeat this step on the other two boards; then stain the edges. When the stain has dried, apply satin polyurethane to the entire table.

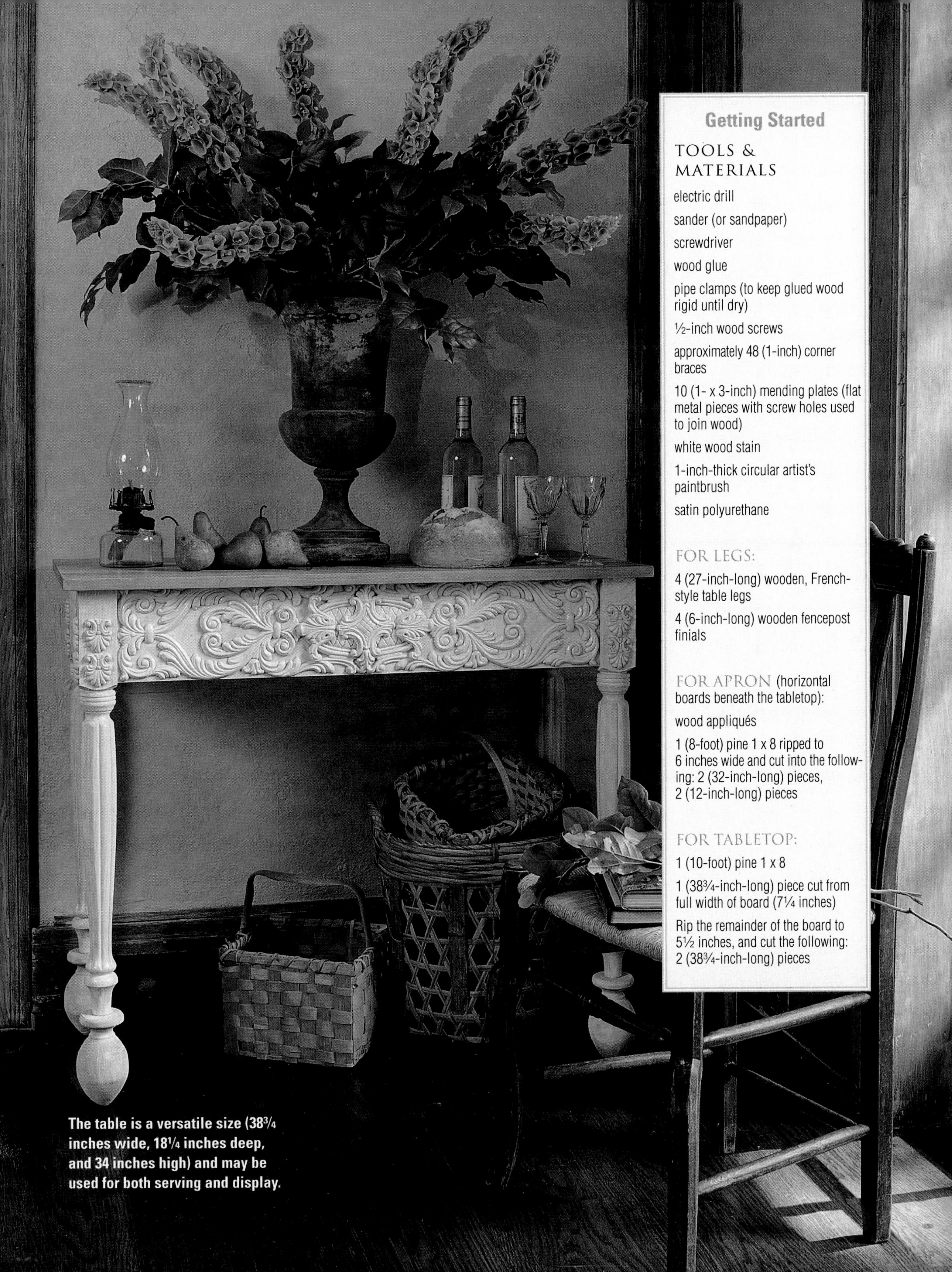

The table is a versatile size ($38^3/_4$ inches wide, $18^1/_4$ inches deep, and 34 inches high) and may be used for both serving and display.

Getting Started

TOOLS & MATERIALS

electric drill

sander (or sandpaper)

screwdriver

wood glue

pipe clamps (to keep glued wood rigid until dry)

½-inch wood screws

approximately 48 (1-inch) corner braces

10 (1- x 3-inch) mending plates (flat metal pieces with screw holes used to join wood)

white wood stain

1-inch-thick circular artist's paintbrush

satin polyurethane

FOR LEGS:

4 (27-inch-long) wooden, French-style table legs

4 (6-inch-long) wooden fencepost finials

FOR APRON (horizontal boards beneath the tabletop):

wood appliqués

1 (8-foot) pine 1 x 8 ripped to 6 inches wide and cut into the following: 2 (32-inch-long) pieces, 2 (12-inch-long) pieces

FOR TABLETOP:

1 (10-foot) pine 1 x 8

1 (38¾-inch-long) piece cut from full width of board (7¼ inches)

Rip the remainder of the board to 5½ inches, and cut the following: 2 (38¾-inch-long) pieces

WEEKEND WORKSHOP

ALL THAT GLITTERS

step 1

step 2

Take a shine to this trim table made from everyday items.

You can create a stylish end table with components purchased at a lumberyard and hardware store. Make the table legs from wooden dowels; then attach them to a plywood circle with metal angle plates. Give the top an unusual paint treatment, using squares of adhesive-backed shelf paper to create a grid as you apply spray paint. A surprise is the crisp metallic edging, made by attaching plain weather stripping to the plywood with bronze upholstery nails.

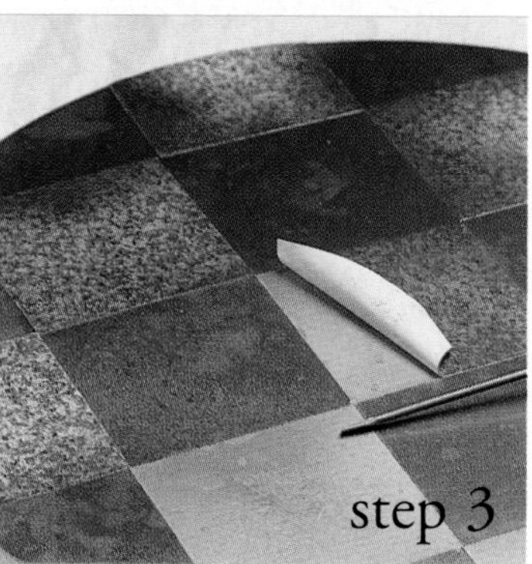
step 3

STEP-BY-STEP

1 PLACE the three angle leg plates on the underside of the birch plywood circle. Imagine it's a clockface, and position the plates at ten, two, and six o'clock, about 3 inches from the edge of the plywood. Drill pilot holes for the screws. Attach leg plates to wood with screws.

2 BRUSH gold paint over right side of plywood circle, and let it dry. Cut adhesive-backed shelf paper into 4-inch squares. Remove paper backing from one square at a time; apply squares (sticky side down) to painted plywood circle, arranging squares in a grid. Spray a light coat of copper spray paint onto plywood.

3 REMOVE squares from painted surface. Use a screwdriver to peel back edge of shelf paper, if necessary. Distress paint with light sanding, if you wish. Apply a coat of polyurethane.

4 MEASURE circumference of tabletop, and add 2 inches. Cut a piece of weather stripping to this measurement; match end to table edge. (Top edge of weather stripping should be even with right side of tabletop.) Tack a bronze upholstery nail through weather stripping. Attach remainder by inserting nails at regular intervals around tabletop.

5 SHORTEN dowels to 26 inches. Spray dowels with copper paint. Paint knobs with gold paint. Drill pilot holes in knobs and at both ends of dowels. Using pliers, screw a dowel screw first into each knob; then screw knob into one end of each dowel. Insert hanger bolts in other end of dowels; then screw legs into metal plates on underside of tabletop.

step 4

Getting Started

TOOLS & MATERIALS

- 3 metal angle leg plates, with screws
- 1 (18-inch-diameter) circle of 1-inch birch plywood
- tape measure
- pencil
- drill
- screwdriver
- brush
- gold paint
- scissors
- adhesive-backed shelf paper
- copper spray paint
- sandpaper
- polyurethane
- metal snips
- weather stripping (without nail holes)
- bronze upholstery nails
- saw
- 3 (1¼-inch-diameter) dowels
- 3 (2-inch-diameter) wooden knobs
- 3 (2-inch) dowel screws
- pliers
- 3 hanger bolts

A painted grid of copper and gold squares gleams on this small circular table. Bronze upholstery nails secure its edging of metal weather stripping.

Index

Decorating Step-By-Step, published by *Southern Living*, offers ideas and projects for creative home design. You'll find complete instructions for making and using a wealth of decorative items for every room. In each issue, you'll also visit homes decorated with imagination and personal flair. Information on art, architecture, and antiques is featured, as well. And ideas for the creative preparation and serving of food flavor each issue. *Decorating Step-By-Step* is a newsstand publication, now available each May, August, and November.

Acknowledgments

Stephanie and Bob Armistead
Wendy Wooden Barze
Jane Boatwright
Tony Brown
Molly and Lange Clark
Danah Coester
Mary and David Collum
Mary Catherine Crowe
Cheryl Dalton
Dave Davis
Colleen Duffley
Beth Ervin
Steve Feller
Mary Leigh Fitts
Rebecca Tully Fulmer
Bob Gager
Sharon Montanna Gilkey
Buffy Drennen Hargett
Donna Heil
Anita Holland
Sherrill Holt
Keith James
Mary Lyn H. Jenkins
Neal Johnson
Sidney Johnson
Marjorie H. Johnston
John Kidd
Sandra A. Lynn
Melanie Martin
Jessica and Grover Maxwell
Mary McWilliams
Emily Minton
Helaine Moyse
Murphy-Tynes Interiors, Birmingham
Beth O'Neal
Pate-Meadows Design, Birmingham
Barbara and Philip Post
Nancy Rogers
Sally Sanderson
Kelly Skelton
Cindy Smith
Patrick Tandy
Charlotte Taylor
Joe and Frank Thackston
Eleanor and Jim Thomason
Leslie and Scott Tichenor
Nancy H. Welch
Jarinda S. Wiechman
Linda Woodrum
Ashley Johnson Wyatt
John P. Wyatt

The products pictured on the pages listed below are available through *Southern Living At HOME*™, the direct selling division of Southern Progress Corporation.

For information about how to obtain these products from a *Southern Living At HOME* Consultant near you, please visit our website at *www.southernlivingathome.com.*

pages 6, 25 (top left), 73, 114 (top right and bottom right), 115, 139 (left)